The Multiage Classroom:
A Collection

Edited by
Robin Fogarty

IRI/Skylight Publishing, Inc.
Palatine, Illinois

The Multiage Classroom: A Collection
Second Printing

Published by IRI/Skylight Publishing, Inc.
200 E. Wood Street, Suite 274
Palatine, Illinois 60067
Phone 800-348-4474, 708-991-6300
FAX 708-991-6420

Creative Director: Robin Fogarty
Editors: Liesl Banks-Stiegman, Erica Pochis, Julia E. Noblitt
Type Compositor: Donna Ramirez
Book Designers: Michael Melasi, Bruce Leckie
Production Coordinators: David Stockman, Amy Behrens

Library of Congress Catalog Card Number: 93-80675
Printed in the United States of America
ISBN 0-932935-71-0

0638-3-95
Item number 1194

Table of Contents

The Multiage Classroom: A Collection

A school should not be a preparation for life. A school should be life.—Elbert Hubbard

The multiage, nongraded, continuous progress classroom resembles the family. It contains groupings of children of various ages working and playing together; clusters of youngsters learning from one another, as well as from their own endeavors; and little people fighting, arguing, displaying impatience and frustrations as they learn to tolerate the diversity of others. It is a multitude of abilities, talents, and styles as well as a spectrum of ages. It is the developmentally appropriate, mixed-age classroom, reminiscent of that "one-room schoolhouse" of years gone by.

As with other educational "innovations," the idea swings like a pendulum does. Now, it's in. Now, it's out. Over the years, the concept has taken on a number of names: one-room schoolhouse, multiaged, split classroom, nongraded, mixed-ages, developmentally appropriate, and continuous progress classroom.

Each time this concept is revisited, it is because it seems so child-compatible, so natural, and so appropriate. Now, once again, the call for holistic models of schooling dictates a thorough investigation of more natural groupings of the students themselves. Although multiage, nongraded, continuous progress classrooms are not new ideas, the implementation of these models carries with it several ramifications. To fully explore the implications of the mixed-age classroom, this collection of articles represents a review of the available literature that is readily accessible and easy to evaluate.

Gathered under one cover, the articles are grouped into manageable pieces of information that focus on specific issues and concerns associated with the concept of mixed-age groupings of students. Leading the collection is a section entitled, "Questions and Answers" that addresses the overriding concerns and frequently asked questions about multiage classrooms. Immediately following this section is a further look at concerns, but the selections are filtered through a "Pros and Cons" approach as readers experience the teeter-totter effect of evaluating the benefits and drawbacks of an idea.

The third section brings together a number of pieces that delineate the procedures and practices associated with the multiage, nongraded, continuous progress classrooms. The section entitled "In Practice" exposes the principles and practices that undergird the concept.

The next two sections of the collection profile primary classrooms and offer examples at the intermediate levels as well. Both present actual illustrations of multiage, nongraded, developmentally appropriate classroom to help readers better visualize these learning environments.

Finally, a cluster of assessment articles are included to bring the exploration of the mixed-age classroom full circle—from the initial questions and pros and cons, to principles and practices in actual classrooms, and then to the final question of evaluation and accountability.

Although the book may suggest a bias toward multiage, nongraded, continuous progress classrooms, the specific articles in the collection are selected to represent an unbiased exploration of the issues. This assortment of ideas may, indeed, answer your most pressing questions and allow you to move ahead with an initiation plan, or it may merely act to open a floodgate of further issues to investigate. In either case, it is our hope that the collection is a stepping stone on the path to schools that are more learner-centered, schools that enable all students to develop and grow to their fullest.

Questions and Answers

I can evade questions without help; what I need is answers.
—John F. Kennedy

As the multiage, nongraded, continuous progress classroom begins to appear on the educational agenda again, questions from parents, staff, and community leaders also arise. After all, change is slow to come; to move from the status quo carries with it concerns about what, why, and how.

In this opening section, two articles, one lengthy and pondering, the other brief and pragmatic are presented. Both are grounded in historic evidence and personal experiences and both offer umbrella overviews of the concept of mixed-aged classes.

Connell's article, "The First 30 Years Were the Fairest: Notes from the Kindergarten and Ungraded Primary (K-1-2)," traces the history of schooling from Sputnik to the late '80s. The author explores the dilemmas of early childhood education: "Nursery schools or not? Five years old by June? September? Or sooner?… Half- or full-day kindergarten? Formal reading or the gradual emergence of literacy…" and exposes the essence of her argument, "We are causing young children to experience school failure." The educational system has neglected the developmental needs of young children and increased the difficulty of the curriculum.

The call to change "the unfortunate lock-step system…designed long, long ago" evolves through a comprehensive look at the function of kindergarten; the age-oriented K-1-2 calendar; the British and New Zealand alternatives; and the author's extensive personal experiences. Connell discusses her wealth of experience from incorporating Montessori methodologies in her multiage, bilingual classrooms to leading the Head Start Program, and influencing the setting of state guidelines in California.

In the second essay, the questions are less theoretical and more practical. "It worked back in the days of the one-room schoolhouse, and it still works today," according to author Kay D. Woelfel. When instituting dual-age classrooms, she believes, "…a principal should be prepared to answer questions like these:…What is it? Why do we need it? How are the teachers and students selected? What is the instructional program? How do students react? How do we know it's successful?"

Both authors speak from experience. There are valuable insights we can learn from their work with multiage groups.

The First 30 Years Were the Fairest

Notes from the Kindergarten and Ungraded Primary (K-1-2)

by Donna Reid Connell

Can we learn anything of value from this richly experienced expert teacher's thoughts and findings?

Exactly 30 years ago, in 1957, the Soviets blasted the first successful manmade satellite—Sputnik—into outer space. A panicked American public pointed an accusing finger at the schools for letting our country "fall behind" in the space race. (Someone quipped, I read, I've forgotten who, that Sputnik's significance was only that Russia's German scientist was a day or two ahead of America's German scientist.) Schools responded to the severe and somewhat hysterical criticism by making curriculum more difficult. Content was moved down, year by year, grade by grade. This change in the primary grades has, for the past 30 years, remained permanent.

Within 5 years after Sputnik, the entire second grade curriculum had been moved into first grade. Children at this grade level (not necessarily at this *developmental* level, of course) were then expected to learn in 1 year what had formerly been taught in 2. The records show that during the past 30 years not a few children have failed to thrive with these sharply higher, and often inappropriate, expectations. Potentially eager little learners have floundered and "failed" first grade!

MANY WAYS TO EASE THE PAIN HAVE BEEN TRIED

It has become increasingly common in the last few years for sophisticated parents who are aware of how inappropriately difficult the first-grade curriculum is to keep their children *home* an

From *Young Children*, vol. 42, no. 5, p. 30–39, 1987. Reprinted with permission extra year. These parents enroll their children in kindergarten 1 year later than their school district's starting age policy permits, so that the children will be a year older when they reach first grade. Thus, the parents hope, the children will be better able to cope.

The kindergarten and first grade as they were during the 30 years between the 1920s and the 1950s—during which period education for young children became more child-centered than it was before the progressives, or has been since the push for "back to basics"—seem to many educated parents and to many educators to have been more fair to children than are the super-pressure programs we have seen more and more of during this most *recent* 30 years.

Humane educators have tried various ways of coping with the casualties of a too-difficult curriculum. Better yet, various ways of preventing bewildered young children from "failing" have been invented.

> Humane educators have tried various ways of coping with the casualties of a too-difficult curriculum.

Some school districts have added an extra year after kindergarten with a name such as *senior kindergarten, transition,* or *transitional first.*

Some school districts have spotted children very early who look likely to "fail" first grade, and have added for them a year *before* kindergarten—*junior kindergarten, developmental kindergarten,* or *preK.*

Some school boards refuse to assume the expense of an extra school year for children identified as *needing* something extra, so label them *learning handicapped,* which makes the district eligible for additional state or federal funding. If young or immature children (or children lacking the kinds of experiences, especially language- and print-rich experiences, that correlate with school success) are *called* young or immature children, they are not eligible for special aid, and their district itself must foot the bill for a year of enrichment. School districts almost always perceive themselves as short of funds, hence the intentional mislabeling of young learners to make their school systems eligible for aid. The intent is to help the children.

The majority of our nation's schools have provided some measure of relief for struggling first graders by moving part of the double whammy curriculum down to the kindergarten, especially reading and writing upper- and lower-case letters, beginning phonics, forming and reading numerals, reading number words, and some number tasks.

Too often today's kindergarten teachers are issued, against their better judgment, the workbooks to go with a specific K-6 or K-8 program adopted by their school or district. Elementary principals sometimes pride themselves on their "articulated" curriculum. This means using the same publisher's wares throughout the school. Often the kindergarten component of these K-6 or K-8 programs has been developed by individuals with little or no current teaching experience in today's kindergartens. (This can be checked by researching the credentials of the listed authors.) The results are often watered-down first grade tasks, only with more cutesy pictures and larger print for younger children.

Textbook Publishers Are Not Helping
Educational publishers, naturally eager to profit, are as eager to profit from this trend as any other, so have produced more and more workbooks and ditto master books to help usually well-meaning teachers help usually agreeable kindergartners learn that which is of secondary importance for them to learn anyway.

Learning letters and numbers through seemingly endless paper-and-pencil skill drills is of secondary importance for 5-year-olds because there are things of far greater importance for them to learn. It isn't that kindergartners can't learn letters and numbers—most of them can and do, though nationally a large percentage don't, and "fail" kindergarten. We wonder just exactly how this teaches *love of learning*, a major curriculum goal in the early years.

For 5-year-olds, it is of far greater importance to share a rich variety of experiences—play; discovery science projects; music, art, and wonderful stories; lively activity-oriented social studies units; frequent outings and small trips; cooperative ventures; and sharing toys, materials, news, and views—all of which should include discussion, discussion, discussion; all of which can involve verbal and written plans, lists, labels, recipes, experience charts, individual stories, and so forth. There is no end to the lengths a conscientious kindergarten teacher can go to with this. It is not even necessary to be creative, only to extend everything a child is doing in every possible sensible and meaningful direction and get it written down for her to see, for him to hear you read.

One of the most significant activities for developing the foundations of literacy in the early years is drawing. A 1981 study of dyslexics at Harvard Medical School revealed a consistent brain pattern for those individuals (McKean, 1981). The study showed evidence of inactivity in the part of the brain that helps plan complicated motor activities. Would time set aside in kindergarten for daily drawing help activate this area of the brain for future writing?

Drawing also builds visual imagery for lab reading comprehension. As an *expressive* activity, drawing balances the many *receptive* activities imposed by many current kindergarten curricula.

WHAT IS THE FUNCTION OF THE KINDERGARTEN?

During the 30 years before Sputnik, one of the main purposes of kindergartens was to provide young children's first group experiences outside the home. Children were made to feel comfortable and confident in school, competent. Conversation was welcome. Children were shown how to tie shoes; remove and get into jackets; recognize their names; memorize their addresses and telephone numbers; take turns; line up; listen to stories; and sit on the floor in a circle, legs folded Indian style. The best kindergartens resembled the model described in this journal [*Young Children*, vol. 42, no. 5, 1987] (pages 12-19) in the article entitled "The Function of the Kindergarten." Regardless of the degree of excellence of the particular kindergarten class, few children failed.

It was taboo during these decades to expose kindergarten children to print. It was supposedly bad for their developing eyes to do so, a strain on their eyes. (In the '80s we don't seem to mind at all "straining their eyes," pencil-steering hands, and tolerance for frustration.) There are times when good educators should ignore nonsense, at whichever end of the pendulum swing it occurs, and, within reason, stick to their convictions. Therefore, I once put signs, *BOYS* and *GIRLS*, on the bathroom doors in my kindergarten. One afternoon after school, my principal entered the room and pointed out these offending signs to a supervisor who accompanied her. The signs were ripped down. Before morning I replaced them with pictures of a boy and a girl. The following day a little boy pointed out the change and asked, "Why can't we put *MEN* and *WOMEN* on the doors like they do at the gas station?"

Educators of that earlier era may not have thought it appropriate for children even to be passively exposed to words in their environment, but children thought it appropriate. As all the recent research on emerging literacy has shown us, it is through stress-free but regular informal exposure to print that each child becomes ready to read.

Why are we educators so extreme? Why is it forbidden to allow children to see written words in one era, and required in the next to drill them relentlessly in reading skills?

Early childhood professionals know instinctively, as well as through their training, that it is primarily not *what* you teach, but *how* you teach that makes for success or failure. More than 50 years of solid child development research tells us strongly that children under a mental age of 6 years— which many 7-year-olds still are too—are usually still in the learn-by-doing stage. They learn to distinguish letters and numerals by handling plastic or wooden models, by trying to make these symbols out of clay, and by twisting their bodies into these shapes. The young child is the center of his own universe. He must "get inside" the content before he knows it. When the young child tries to write a word or sentence, she must first say each speech sound in sequence as she forms the letters. Early composition is a noisy process. We must question whether or not a kindergarten or first grade (or even a second grade) without a great many lively play activities and interesting projects, and a great deal of quiet conversation among children, is functioning appropriately.

> It is primarily not *what* you teach, but *how* you teach that makes for success or failure.

WHAT IS WRONG? HOW DID OUR K-1-2 GET SO CALENDAR AGE-ORIENTED? ARE THERE ALTERNATIVES?

In recent years more and more articles have appeared concerning the problems of teaching the youngest children in today's kindergartens. Many teachers recommend raising the entrance age for beginners so they can better master the prescribed curriculum. Would raising entrance age make a difference? Minimum entrance age in the United States varies from 4 years old in New Jersey to 5 by September 1 in 10 states. Other states are in between. The problem is obviously not with entrance age, but that some children in a class are older than others. Some children are chronologically older. Is it not natural that sometimes the younger children will have difficulty keeping up with the older ones? Would we expect the same performance of 1-year-olds as of 2s, of 2-year-olds as of 3s, of 4-year-olds as of 5s? Why then do we expect the same performance of 5s in kindergarten (those just turning 5 during the summer) as of 6s (those who have been 5 since shortly after September 1 a year ago)? Other children are not chronologically older, but are older developmentally speaking, or seem younger than others of the same birth date age.

> We are still acting as if all we know about children is what is on their birth certificates.

Around the beginning of this century our nation was receiving numbers of immigrants from all over the world. School administrators in the big cities had to assign the hordes of new children to suitable learning groups. Little was known about the children's backgrounds, native languages, or former education. The solution? Aha! We would divide them into classes by their birth certificates! The graded school model was born. It is still the major model for grouping schoolchildren in the United States. We are still acting as if all we know about children is what is on their birth certificates. Age on September 1 is usually the determinant for entrance to school. That date was selected because it was near the end of the summer harvest season. We are still acting as if we were primarily an agricultural nation. The age-graded pattern is so common that any variation from it called *alternative.*

The common national practice here today segregates school entrants into 12-month blocks. Regardless of the established age at entrance, the current system covers children whose accumulated life experiences vary from 1 to 12 months. The general public and the educational establishment assume that all these children have equal opportunity to learn the same prescribed curriculum. If some children do not progress satisfactorily, it is assumed that the children have failed, rather than that the system has failed to meet their needs. No matter how this is presented to the child or the family, the child is separated from the other children who move on. The child feels different from her classmates. At age 5 or 6 it does not help the self-concept. To avoid this trauma, kindergarten teachers are humanely suggesting that we raise entrance age. Is this not manipulating children to solve an administrative problem?

The Supreme Court has emphatically stated that it is unconstitutional to segregate children by sex, race, ethnic, or socioeconomic differences. Young children have no control over these, or over their own month of conception or birth. If their accumulated months of life have an effect on their future success in school, then should it not also be unconstitutional to continue a system in our schools whereby month of birth gives some children a distinct advantage and some a definite disadvantage? It is a break in our national code of civil rights.

Two Alternatives

Is there an alternative method of grouping the youngest children in school—those younger than 8? Are 12-month blocks for beginners necessary? Have other groupings been tried?

During World War II, many young British children were sent away from their parents to live in areas less likely to be bombed. After the war, when children returned home, to help heal the children's emotional scars, *British educators created primary schools with new social patterns; they called classes* family groupings. The term means that, as in a family, children are of different ages and therefore there are different expectations for each child. Children in these schools were divided, not into 12-month blocks, but into more natural 3-year groups (ages 4-5-6, 5-6-7, 6-7-8). Students stayed with the same familiar teacher for several years. When some of the older children showed that they were ready to move on, some new younger children moved into the group. The formerly younger children then automatically became senior in the group. Sometimes siblings were in the same group, giving security to both children. Older children helped teach younger ones. These British primary schools were not unlike our own American one-room schools.

Here is another alternative: *New Zealand permits children to enter school any time during the school year on their fifth birthday.* At first these children are called *early entrants.* They move through several cycles or steps during that first year at their own pace. Forward movement is only by achievement, not by birthday, or because the whole class is "being promoted" in a block consisting of children with birthdays dotted throughout a span of 12 months. There is no "skipping"—and there is no "failure." (I have visited New Zealand schools myself, and have talked with educators. They cannot imagine our system. To them, it seems so unfair to young children.) The major advantage of their system, New Zealanders feel, is that no one expects the newcomer to function academically at the same level as the children who entered months before—as the children who are months older. Differences are expected and celebrated as each child joins the school community on her birthday.

MY PERSONAL EXPERIENCES TEACHING UNGRADED *K–1–2*

To help solve the current controversies relating to kindergarten age at entrance and the curriculum imposed on kindergartners and first and second graders by outside forces, we might reflect on our own nation's one- and two-room schools, most of which have disappeared. What can we learn from them?

Background

Following our own trauma of World War II, my husband and I searched for a low-stress environment in which to raise our family. We moved to a ranch in Napa Valley, California. Three of our four children were of preschool age. In order to broaden their social experiences we joined with our neighbors in establishing a play group. In several years this grew to a full-blown parent cooperative preschool. With this teaching experience I was later drafted into teaching in a rural one-room school for 18 children.

> Differences are expected and celebrated as each child joins the school community on her birthday.

On the first morning I rang the antique hand-held brass bell to signal the beginning of class. As the students filed in from the playground an additional 10 children of various ages joined us from the nearby vineyards. They were children of the migrant workers. None of them spoke English. Instantly, I became not only a teacher of a multigrade group, but a bilingual teacher as well.

Until harvest season was over 6 weeks later, we communicated with our Spanish-speaking students primarily by physical demonstrations. Instead of telling them what to do, the other students and I *showed* them, an approach taught to educators years ago by Dr. Maria Montessori. My preschool background in learn-by-doing activities helped. We had no prescribed curriculum for teaching a bilingual class, and no materials. We improvised. My junior high Spanish gradually returned. When the migrant children moved on all of us were minimally bilingual.

My bilingual teaching experience led to directing our county's first Head Start program. While recruiting children we discovered three distinct minority groups in our valley. One minority was the children of single mothers who were supported by Aid to Families with Dependent Children (AFDC) funds. Another minority was the children of the vineyard workers, whose home language was Spanish. Then we discovered a third minority. They were English-speaking children who lived on isolated ranches. At the end of the summer we administered a simple test to find out if we had been able to make a difference in these three groups of children. The group that had made the least progress was the isolated group. The children's problem was undeveloped language. Language and thinking skills go hand in hand. Because they had no neighborhood playmates, these children's language was significantly below age expectation.

Our Two-Room Primary School

Following my Head Start work with the school district, I was assigned to a two-room primary school. Soda Canyon School was located at the entrance to a pocket canyon 10 miles long. Families who lived at the farthest corners of the canyon rarely came over the narrow mountain road to town. These children exhibited the same undeveloped language as the Head Start children. On the other hand, schoolchildren whose families lived at the mouth of the canyon had developed mature language through frequent neighborhood play experiences. This language spread caused wide differences in achievement.

I was assigned to teach the younger children, kindergarten and first-grade age. My teammate for the second- and third-grade students was fresh from college and open to innovation. We began to share classes. She came into my room to teach math while I took her older group for writing activities. We discovered that some of the older students, particularly those from isolated families, were at the same academic levels as the younger group.

We were teaching the same content twice—inefficient. We regrouped the students by achievement levels. Following the British primary model, no group had an age spread of more than 3 years. By adapting to the children's needs, we gradually evolved into a departmentalized, ungraded primary school.

The neighbors at the far end of the canyon reported that there was an 8-year-old boy who had never been to school. The county attendance officer was driven away by shots from the boy's father's shotgun. The school nurse then put on her white coat and bravely approached the ranch. She convinced the family that the boy should come to school. The following week when his 18-year-old sister brought him she told us that she had not been to school for 10 years. Through a work-study program, we were able to hire her as our aide. She proved to be a valuable playground director, nature study expert, and art teacher. She learned basic academic skills with our primary students.

To answer parents' questions about our alternative program, we asked them to an evening meeting. The standing room only crowd was bigger than that for the annual Christmas program. To get support from parents, alternative educational programs must be fully explained to them. We invited parents to visit whenever they came by the school on the way to town. And they did! Many of these adults had previously led groups of children in 4-H activities. They were comfortable in a teaching role. They read stories to children, listened to beginners read, brought in farm animals to share, and supervised learning games. Visitors sometimes commented, "This school looks like a parent cooperative preschool!" Our considerable parent involvement was a direct outgrowth of my own experience both in a parent cooperative preschool and in Head Start. We had parent involvement in full measure. To achieve that, teachers must really want parents and really help them participate significantly in the program.

> **To get support from parents, alternative educational programs must be fully explained to them.**

One year the state widened the highway adjoining the school. Instead of letting the noisy earth-moving equipment disturb our teaching, we sat on the bank and watched. We had a first-hand social studies and science program. The children then brought their own realistic Tonka™ earth-moving toys to school. The local Caterpillar tractor agency provided us with other model equipment. The children set up their own earth-moving project in our sandbox. Together, for 3 months, the children and I translated everything the children played into drawings, charts, chalkboard readings, and homemade books. Reading skills can be taught using anything in writing.

My role as the major language arts teacher was to find a successful way to teach reading and writing to the children whose oral language was below age expectation. All the phonics programs available used the concept of beginning sounds of key words (*b* is for ball). Many of the rural children could extract ending sounds of words, but not beginnings. I then invented a phonics program using sounds made by animals familiar to the rural children, rather than the names of the animals—The mosquito hums/mmm/; The hound dog pants/hhhh/. This program gives children the skills for writing creative compositions with inventive spelling before they read books. All the student activities are traditional early childhood activities: listening to stories, acting out the stories through dramatic play, drawing the animal characters, and moving like the animals.

A group of mothers made a set of 26 beanbags in the shape of the letter-animals. The beginners learned to blend the animal sounds together into words through beanbag tossing games. It worked! (When Right to Read from the U.S. Office Education made a nationwide search for "Effective Reading Programs," our beanbag program was selected as one of the few original approaches for teaching sound-symbol correspondence. Other selections were effective use of commercial programs.)

One day we were playing a pass-it-on whispering game. I noticed the pained expressions on the faces of our rural children whose articulation was so poor. They were giving the game extreme extra effort. I realized that these children could not whisper! Most of their communication was in vowel sounds. With whispering, consonants are emphasized and vowel sounds are suppressed. We added to our curriculum a daily lip-reading game, with exaggerated mouth positions. Articulation dramatically improved. This spilled over into better test scores for these children. Every child played the game. Those with poor articulation were never singled out.

My teammate brought in a plastic bowling set. A parent donated a strip of hall carpeting to reduce the noise. Voilà! An ideal game for introducing the concept of subtraction was born. Practicing combinations up to 10 in a motivating context became a major pastime.

We set aside the last hour for reviewing the events of each school day. The youngest children drew a picture about the day to share at home. They told us about their picture to help develop oral language. Every day the older children developed an experience story to summarize our day. Instead of having the students copy the story, we dictated it to all children who could write. This was word by word, encouraging children to "write with their ears." We told parents that we believed this invented spelling would eventually lead the children to be good spellers. These daily messages demonstrated to parents that some actual learning was going on. Our writing exercise thus became our public relations program. Five years later we did a comparative study to find out if our unusual approach to spelling had worked. In fifth grade, the children taught spelling first by ear while in first grade had significantly higher scores in spelling on the Stanford Achievement Test than the district norm.

OUR LITTLE SCHOOL INFLUENCED STATE GUIDELINES
One year an intern student from the University of California was assigned to us. Her supervisor later was secretary to the California task force that developed the state's exemplary early childhood education program.

The state design included these major changes that the secretary had observed at our Soda Canyon School:
- Departmentalized staffing
- Multiage grouping
- Paraprofessional aides
- Parent involvement
- Peer tutoring
- Objectives based on diagnosis of student needs

- Individualized instruction (meaning not one-to-one, but appropriate)
- School climate that enhances self-concept
- Opportunity for a child to complete the 4-year primary curriculum in 3, 4, or 5 years without being considered exceptional.

Family grouping permitted newly entering children from our area's Spanish-speaking culture to experience much less separation anxiety because they were with siblings until they were comfortable in the school setting. With no grade levels at Soda Canyon, no child was officially retained or accelerated. No child moved to fourth grade at the larger school until readiness for success was obvious. The extra year to grow was all that was necessary. To me, the best groupings a school can have vary, but are 4–5–6, or 5–6–7, or 6–7–8, or 7–8–9; usually third graders have more in common with fourth than with second graders. When asked what grade they were in, a common answer from the Soda Canyon children was "I don't know. I go to Primary School."

Is It Any Harder to Teach an Ungraded Group? Does It Work Better?

In most American schools today, by third grade most classroom rosters will reveal a spread of 3 years, not 12 months. Along the way some children have been retained, and some accelerated. Both decisions result in trauma for the individuals involved.

Grouping in K–1–2 spans is no different, except the differences are considered natural and normal.

Is it harder to teach a 3-year span, such as K–1–2? It is common practice to divide a primary class into three reading or math groups for efficient teaching. One group is usually working above the grade designation and one below—a 3-year span. Grouping in K–1–2 spans is no different, except the differences are considered natural and normal. There is no "dumb" group. (Anyone who thinks children in the lowest reading group don't feel dumb doesn't know young children well.) And, like the one-room school, there is an atmosphere of cooperation, rather than competition.

It took no extra funding to run our Soda Canyon Ungraded Primary School. We simply

1. grouped students in a fashion more consistent with the philosophy of enhancing each child's positive self-image than the arbitrary 12-month block system typically used, and

2. instead of designing a curriculum and then trying to fit children into it, we design a developmental curriculum around the specific needs of individual enrolled children. *With these two changes our end-of-year achievement scores went from next to the lowest of 24 elementary schools in the district to the highest.*

Parents from other schools began to enroll their children with us until we were filled to our capacity of 60 students. Parents camped out all night on the school grounds to be among the first in line on enrollment day. Our success was not appreciated by the other elementary principals who used the traditional age-graded system. Five years after we started this work, when the district's enrollment dropped, the principals convinced the school board that larger schools are more economical. This may be true in a certain sense, but not when the immense cost of remediation and retention are considered—not to mention the cost to society of causing children to become so discouraged that they drop out and become the unemployed, underemployed, or those with very expensive problems such as drug problems. Political pressure then forced the board to close our model school.

SHOULD WE ORGANIZE AND ADVOCATE FOR BETTER WAYS TO BEGIN CHILDREN'S SCHOOL YEARS?

As an individual child advocate, I failed to make a permanent change in my school district. Group action by parents, backed by early childhood professionals, however, might be sufficient political clout to encourage school boards to experiment with better ways to group children in their first years of school.

Nursery school or not? Five years old by June? September? Or sooner? Gesell tests or developmental screening? Half- or full-day kindergarten? Formal reading readiness, or the gradual emergence of literacy through exposure to loved ones, reading and writing at home and elsewhere, being read to frequently, and seeing admired people reading and writing throughout their lives? These are all important questions, but we have another centrally important issue to focus on, too.

We are *causing* young children to experience all the lowered self-esteem, loss of friends, parental concern, and damaged motivation that comes from school failure. Perhaps the solution to the problem will come, not by manipulating children with regard to birth dates and extra classes, but by changing the unfortunate lock-step system that we designed long, long ago.

BIBLIOGRAPHY

Barth, R. S. (1972). *Open education and the American school.* New York: Agathon.

Blackie, J. (1971). *Inside the primary school.* New York: Schocken.

Bloom, B. S. (1976). *Human characteristics and school learning.* New York: McGraw-Hill.

Bremer, A., & Bremer, J. (1972). *Open education: A beginning.* New York: Holt, Rinehart & Winston.

Clay, M. M. (1975). *What did I write?* Aukland, New Zealand: Heinemann Educational Books.

Cratty, B. J. (1971). *Active learning: Games to enhance academic abilities.* Englewood Cliffs, NJ: Prentice-Hall.

Gartner, A., Kohler, M., & Reissman, F. (1971). *Children teach children.* New York: Harper & Row.

Goodlad, J. I. (1962). *Some propositions in search of schools.* Washington, DC: NAEYC.

Gross, B., & Gross, R. (1974). *Will it grow in a classroom?* New York: Delacorte.

Hertzberg, A., & Stone, E. F. (1971). *Schools are for children: An American approach to the open classroom.* New York: Schocken.

Lee, D. M., & Allen, R. V. (1963). *Learning to read through experience* .(2nd ed.). New York: Meredith Corporation.

Lembo, J. M. (1972). *When learning happens.* New York: Schocken.

Maccoby, E. E., & Zellner, M. (1970). *Experiments in primary education: Aspects of Project Follow-Through.* New York: Harcourt Brace Jovanovich.

Murrow, C., & Murrow, L. (1971). *Children come first: The inspired work of English primary schools.* New York: American Heritage.

Ridgway, L., & Lawton, I. (1965). *Family grouping the primary school.* New York: Agathon.

Rudolph, M. (1973). *From hand to head.* New York: McGraw-Hill.

Schwebel, M., & Raph, J. (1973). *Piaget in the classroom.* New York: Basic.

Silberman, M. L., Allender, J. S., & Yanoff, J. M. (1972). *The psychology of open teaching and learning: An inquiry approach.* Boston: Little Brown.

Smith, L. L. (1968). *A practical approach to the nongraded elementary school.* West Nyack, NY: Parker.

Spodek, B. (1970). *Open education.* Washington, DC: NAEYC.

Tewksbury, J. L. (1967). *Nongrading in the elementary school.* Columbus, OH: Merrill.

Weber, L. (1971). *The English infant school and informal education.* Englewood Cliffs, NJ: Prentice-Hall.

Wolsch, R. A., & Wolsch, L. A. C. (1970). *From speaking to writing to reading: Relating the arts of communication.* New York: Teachers College Press, Columbia University.

REFERENCES

Connell, D. R. (1985). *itl, Early Writing Program.* Circle Pines, MN: American Guidance Service. (Originally published 1978 by Academic Therapy Publications, Novato, California, as *The Integrated Total Language Program*).

McKean, K. (1981, December). Beaming new light on the brain. *Discover,* pp. 30–31.

Right to Read Effort. (1975). *Effective Reading Programs.* Urbana, IL: National Council of Teachers of English.

The Dual-Age Classroom
Questions and Answers
by Kay D. Woelfel

It worked back in the days of the one-room schoolhouse, and it still works today.

A split is a split is a split—except when you call it a dual-age class. That's when a principal should be prepared to answer questions like these from staff, students, and parents.

What is a dual-age class? This is an organizational plan in which students from two grade levels are grouped together.

Why do you need a dual-age class? When enrollment fluctuates, dual-age classes are an effective means of maintaining a reasonable student/teacher ratio. Let's say that your school board budgets for 24:1 class size and you have sixty students in grade four and sixty in grade five. You can divide the sixty students in each grade into two oversize classes of thirty each. Or you can make two classes of twenty-four each, and combine the "left-overs" in each grade into a dual-age class of twelve fourth graders and twelve fifth graders.

How is the teacher selected? If ever there was a linchpin, here it is. A teacher must have experience, flexibility, and creativity to lead a dual-age class. It's hard work. Look for a teacher skilled in planning and organizing total group activities, as well as small group and individualized instruction. It's a good idea to hire an instructional aide so that the student/instructor ratio is less than that of the single-age classroom.

From *Principal*, vol. 71, no. 3, p. 32–33, January 1992. Reprinted with permission.

How are the students selected? Carefully. Students who can work both cooperatively and independently usually succeed in a dual-age class, and you can use staff and parent input to identify good candidates. When all is said and done, the chronological ages and achievement ranges are usually narrower than those in the "straight" classes.

What kind of instructional program is offered? Students continue to move through the subject area content and skills in the usual sequence. Thematic approaches lend themselves nicely to science and social studies, creating an opportunity for whole-class instruction. (Alternate units can be used to ensure that students who return to a traditional class the next year don't repeat the curriculum.) Reading, language arts, and math are taught at appropriate instructional levels.

How do parents react? Many parents are pleased, because they see the dual-age class as an opportunity for their child to have a highly qualified teacher and a smaller student/teacher ratio. Parents of younger students see their children challenged by the pace of their older classmates. A legitimate concern of parents might be that a physically mature older child might seem threatening to younger and smaller children. On the other hand, parents of older students need to be reassured that their children will be challenged academically, that they will receive grade-appropriate instruction, and that every component of the grade-level curriculum will also be covered in the dual-age classroom.

It's important to give the whys and wherefores of dual-age instruction to students as well as parents and staff.

One word of caution. Older students placed in a dual-age class may view the placement as a form of retention, creating negative feelings for the student and family.

How do students react? It's important to give the whys and wherefores of dual-age instruction to students as well as parents and staff. In the spring, after assignment plans take shape, students should be informed about the proposed dual-age class—what it is and what it isn't. Most lower-grade kids will like the idea of participating with older kids, but some older students may view it as "working with babies" and fear teasing by their peers. A little counseling can go a long way to curb those feelings.

Are dual-age classes as successful as single-age classes? Both types work well, and there are more similarities than differences. Both have comparable ranges of age, achievement level, and behavior. Both have curriculums designed to meet the needs of their children.

How can a principal know if a dual-age class is successful? Just ask. A principal can take the pulse of a dual-age class by making frequent contact with the parents, students, and teacher, especially during the first week of school. This will give the kind of feedback necessary to make any adjustments in placements, curriculum, teacher assistance, schedules, or materials.

Yes, a split is a split is a split, but the decision to create a dual-age class need not divide staff, parents, or students. Dual-age classes are effective, and they can be the answer to keeping reasonable class sizes during periods of fluctuating enrollments.

REFERENCES

Hogue, J. and Simmons, B. "Sidestep the Pitfalls of Combined Classes." *The Executive Educator* (September 1984): 24.

Slavin, R. "Synthesis of Research on Grouping in Elementary and Secondary Schools." *Educational Leadership* (September 1988): 67-77.

Section 2

The Pros and Cons

All great ideas are controversial, or have been at one time.
—George Seldes

"In virtually every argument for restructuring American schools, there are either explicit references to the rigidity and inappropriateness of the conventional graded structure, or implicit recommendations for continuous progress and changes in present promotion/retention practices," so begins Anderson's essay in this section that examine the pros and cons of the nongraded classroom. As he cites Dewey's vision of "educating the whole child," Anderson obviously takes a strong position in favor of the nongraded models and discusses some of the "habits" that are holding us back from implementing them.

In a more balanced perspective, Lodish discusses the pluses and minuses of mixed-age groupings. The benefits of multiage grouping he cites include: opportunities for students to develop relationships with others who match, complement, or supplement their own needs; greater cooperation; effectiveness in dealing with different rates of development; and stimulation for intellectual growth. On the other hand, the cons of mixed-age grouping Lodish outlines involve: difficulty in finding same-age, same-sex friends; the possibility that older students are not challenged; frustration of younger students; scheduling problems, and the necessity for more intensive planning on the part of the teachers.

A third essay focuses on the merits of the multiage classroom and settles the perennial debate. Addressing the theme of children's friendships, Pratt concludes that "the general picture that emerges…is one of increased competition and aggression within same-age groups and increased harmony and nurturance within multiage groups." Pratt also states that "situations with cross-generational friendships in high schools, in which adults are enrolled, also yield positive findings."

In addition to positive findings on vocabulary development, tutoring, benefits to older or younger members of the group and effects on social and emotional development, the author cites results that suggest children and adolescents chose friends who were "on an equivalent level in terms of development rather than chronological age."

An article by Milburn discusses an experiment in multiage grouping that reveals "little difference in basic skills achievement levels, but a big difference in attitudes toward school." He stresses that "the rationale for multiage grouping assumes cognitive benefits…and affective benefits," and concludes that multiage grouping is but "one of the strategies for teaching youngsters."

Another solid essay included is a recent piece about the benefits of nongraded schools as mandated by Kentucky and Oregon. In this article, Pavan defines nongraded as "progress reported in terms of tasks…teams of teachers…students [as] active participants." The author reviews the research findings and suggests favorable patterns for nongraded. Complimenting Pavan's essay, Slavin cites a review of the research with Gutierrez that concludes "that the effectiveness of nongraded elementary programs depends in large part on the features of the program…" Pavan responds with a comment made by Goodlad in "The Nongraded Elementary School" (1987), in which he stresses that it is the "philosophy behind nongradedness…that must infuse much more than merely structure."

Finally, this section debating the pros and cons of nongraded multiage classrooms ends with a brief piece by Cohen. The author states "the most critical variable is the skill of the teacher," when implementing multiage groupings." Furthermore, Cohen believes that the diversity of students in the '90s classroom favors nongradedness because of "a search for school practices designed to accommodate these individual differences."

This section provides fertile ground for public debate on the issues of nongraded schooling. In fact, structuring a live debate among staff, parents, and community leaders based on the readings in this section is a recommended strategy for exposing the issues and concerns surrounding the multiage classroom.

The Return of the Nongraded Classroom

by Robert H. Anderson

Major changes in school structure have created a promising new climate for an old approach to education.

Has the time for nongradedness in elementary schools finally come? My answer is *yes!* There are powerful forces for educational change in this country that are calling for structural as well as instructional improvements that are wholly consistent with nongraded concepts and approaches. The educational environment has rarely been as favorable as it is today.

Nearly every other dimension of restructuring, including teacher empowerment, teamwork, site-based decision making, and providing more flexible alternatives for students, changes the dynamics of school practice in ways that make a nongraded approach not only more meaningful, but also more attainable.

In virtually every argument for restructuring American schools, there are either explicit references to the rigidity and inappropriateness of the conventional graded structure, or implicit recommendations for continuous progress and changes in present promotion/retention practices. Never before in its checkered history has the graded school, with its lockstep curriculum and competitive-comparative pupil evaluation system, come under such attack not only by thoughtful educators, but also by politicians and business people. No less a figure than W. Edwards Deming, the guru of total quality management, has become a vocal critic of school retention, grouping, and competitive grading practices.

From *Principal*, vol. 72, no. 3, p. 9–12, January 1993. Reprinted with permission.

The Trouble with Graded Schools

It is strange that the graded school, with its overloaded, text-book-dominated curriculum, and its relatively primitive assumptions about human development and learning, has held its ground this long. To my knowledge there has never been a respectable body of research or scholarly reflection on the academic and social legitimacy of segregating students by age and providing them with a standard curriculum.

The graded school concept, born of administrative practicality and puritanical traditions, was first introduced by Horace Mann to Massachusetts from Prussia in the mid-nineteenth century. It is unfortunate that these justifications for graded schools persist in the 1990s.

Equally persistent is the historic isolation of predominantly female teachers from each other, often combined with supervisory practices that could be labeled as sexist in today's society, as well as punishment practices that could be labeled as child abuse. Add to this the tendency of many educators and business leaders to continue viewing the tax-supported public school system largely as a funnel for producing unskilled workers at a time when there are no longer an abundance of jobs available to them.

Regrettably, John Dewey's visionary concepts of "educating the whole child" and of appealing to children's multi-dimensional interests and talents failed to gain much momentum until well after World War II. And even today, the use of terms such as "critical thinking," "humane educational practices," or "child-centered classrooms" produce sharply negative reaction in some communities.

Déjà Vu All Over Again?

It is difficult to write an accurate history of nongradedness, partly because there have been so many instances over the years of varied efforts, each with its own label and ground rules, and partly because the extent of success of such efforts were rarely recorded. In the post-Sputnik climate of educational reform, labels such as "nongraded education," "open education," "team teaching," and "individualized instruction" were often used more as expressions of intent than as titles of accomplishment.

However, in many schools and districts across the country, there emerged the forerunners of what is now being defined as nongraded education. The movement began after World War II, when an expanding pupil population produced a corresponding surge of interest in how better to fit schooling practices to emerging understanding of child growth and development. In a climate favorable for "modernizing" schools, a "first wave" of nongradedness began in the 1950s and continued through the early 1970s. In retrospect, however, those early efforts touched only a small fraction of American schoolchildren, and only a few of them led to the establishment of authentic nongraded models.

Therefore, it is inaccurate for any educator to shout "déjà vu!" and to say that nongradedness has already been tried and found wanting. Some fairly good nongraded programs did emerge and thrive over time, notably with the team-taught, multi-aged grouping framework of Individually Guided Education, as developed by the Kettering Foundation and the University of Wisconsin. We are not starting from scratch in the 1990s.

Barbara Pavan, who first surveyed the research literature on nongradedness about 20 years ago, recently completed an update of that research with 64 added studies (Anderson and Pavan 1993). Her findings showed that, in terms of academic achievement and mental health, results favoring graded groups are very rare. Most of the studies show neutral or inconclusve outcomes when graded and nongraded groups are compared, but results favoring the nongraded approach are growing in both quantity and quality.

> In terms of academic achievement and mental health, results favoring graded groups are very rare.

"There is now," Pavan reports, "definitive research evidence to confirm the theories underlying nongradedness." It appears a nongraded environment especially benefits boys, blacks, underachievers, and students from lower socioeconomic groups, with the benefits increasing the longer that children remain in that environment. Pavan's work also confirms the conclusion that nongradedness is most likely to thrive when teachers work in teams with multi-aged aggregations of children.

What's Holding Us Back?

As seems to be true for all efforts at educational reform, the obstacles to nongradedness are mostly matters of habit and attitude. Some of the more constraining *habits* of teachers include:

- Over-reliance on graded instructional materials and tests;
- Voluntary seclusion in self-contained classrooms;
- Reluctance to take risks or rock the boat;
- Familiarity with graded classes from their own childhoods; and
- Disinclination to pursue new skills through staff development.

Some of the most constraining *attitudes*, closely linked with the foregoing habits, are:

- Resentment (often justified) of administrators' tendencies to embrace every innovation that comes along;
- Skepticism about theoretical, as opposed to practical, ideas;
- Limited acceptance of the slogan, proclaimed by Jerome Bruner, Benjamin Bloom, and others, that "all children can learn"; and
- Conviction that some children can only be motivated extrinsically (e.g., by graded report cards and fear of retention).

On the positive side, the great majority of teachers now in service are better educated, particularly with respect to how children develop and learn, than were their predecessors a generation ago. They are more accepting of individual differences and more aware of the vast array of pedagogical options available to them, including whole language, cooperative learning, and heterogeneous grouping.

Similarly, today's principals are better prepared to assume the role of facilitator, and more willing to share decision-making power with their staffs. Both teachers and principals also understand the great need we have in our schools for professional communication and collaboration.

One of the reasons that nongradedness seems more achievable in the 1990s is that there are now good models available for pupil-peer tutoring and cooperative learning programs, as well as a wider variety of technological aids and instructional materials. Authentic nongraded programs can make good use of these models and materials.

Most advocates of nongradedness believe it is essential for students to belong to a basic aggregation of children that embraces at least two (preferably three) age groups. Thus, a nongraded primary group might include five-, six-, and seven-year-olds, or six-, seven-, and eight-year-olds. We now know that the most natural learning environment for children calls for heterogenous multi-age groupings, within which all sorts of homogeneous *and* heterogeneous subgroupings can be created as needed.

I believe that an ideal nongraded grouping should number from 70 to 120 children, in the charge of a team of three to six teachers. It has been demonstrated that a truly nongraded environment is much easier to produce when the philosophy and practices of nongradedness are combined with multi-age approaches and some form of team teaching. In fact, it is almost impossible to find examples of authentic nongradedness within single-age groups of children taught by lone teachers in self-contained classrooms.

What Is Authentic Nongradedness?

Authentic nongraded schools should meet, or come close to meeting, the following criteria:

- Replacement of labels associated with gradedness, like first grade and fifth grade, with group titles like "primary unit" that are more appropriate to the concept of continuous progress;
- Replacement of competitive-comparative evaluation systems (and the report cards associated with them) with assessment and reporting mechanisms that respect continuous individual progress and avoid competitive comparisons;
- All grouping to include at least two heterogeneous age cohorts;
- Groups assembled for instructional purposes to be non-permanent, being dissolved and reconstituted as needed;
- Organization of the teaching staff into teams, with teachers having maximum opportunities to interact and collaborate;
- Development of a flexible interdisciplinary, whole-child-oriented curriculum, with grade-normed books and tests used only as resources (if used at all);
- Adoption of official policies consistent with nongradedness in the school and at the school board level, even where waivers of policy may be required (*e.g.*, reporting enrollments by grades).

Where do you find authentic nongradedness? This is a tough question to answer, for two reasons. First, schools offering programs that can be considered "authentic" (*see box*) are not abundant; and second, there are few accurate listings of these schools should you wish to visit one. The Canadian province of British Columbia probably has the most such schools at the moment, although states like Kentucky and Oregon may soon provide good models. At present, several organizations are cooperating on a project to establish an international registry of such schools, which would serve as models for nongraded education.

How Do You Go Nongraded?

In our 1993 book, Pavan and I propose that one of the first steps should be to take an inventory of your staff's basic beliefs and intuitions. If too many teachers are uncomfortable with the philosophy and practices associated with nongradedness, there is little point in taking the plunge. Conversely, if many on your staff are true believers, mountains can be moved!

The next step is for your teachers to immerse themselves in the literature in order to acquire a sound knowledge base about authentic nongradedness. Such immersion should include the resolution of questions about such matters as pupil grouping, teacher teaming, evaluating pupil progress, dealing with the public, and adopting necessary policies.

Simply launching a nongraded program is at least a two-year process.

You should be forewarned that simply *launching* a nongraded program is at least a two-year process. It takes a lot of time to work out policies and procedures, to make curriculum changes, to prepare the community, and to provide appropriate staff development and training. To develop a mature and smooth-running operation, with an integrated, interdisciplinary, and multi-dimensional curriculum may require an addition five years.

But when it comes to developing an exciting and successful nongraded program, it is well to remember that trite but useful motto: "Rome wasn't built in a day!"

REFERENCES

American Association of School Administrators. *The Nongraded Primary: Making Schools Fit Children.* Arlington, Va.: The Association, 1992.

Anderson, Robert H., and Pavan, Barbara N. *Nongradedness: Helping It to Happen.* Lancaster, Pa.: Technomic Publishing, 1993.

Bloom, Benjamin S. *Human Characteristics and School Learning.* New York: McGraw-Hill, 1976.

Bruner, Jerome S. *The Process of Education.* Cambridge, Mass.: Harvard University Press, 1960.

Gardner, Howard. *Frames of Mind: The Theory of Multiple Intelligences.* New York: Basic Books, 1983.

Gayfer, Margaret. *The Multi-Grade Classroom: Myth and Reality.* Toronto: Canadian Education Association, 1991.

Gaustad, Joan. "Nongraded Education: Mixed-Age, Integrated, and Developmentally Appropriate Education for Primary Children." *OSSC Bulletin* (Oregon School Study Council), March 1992.

Gaustad, Joan. "Making the Transition from Graded to Nongraded Primary Education." *OSSC Bulletin* (Oregon School Study Council), April 1992.

Goodlad, John, I., and Anderson, Robert H. *The Nongraded Elementary School*, 3rd Edition. New York: Teachers College Press, 1987.

The Pros and Cons of Mixed-Age Grouping

by Richard Lodish

There are times when two age groups in a classroom are better than one—and times when they are not.

Multi-age grouping had its roots in the one-room village school which, in an earlier time, combined age groups out of necessity. But in recent years, a number of larger, graded schools have tried to recapture the potential advantages of a wide age range in their classrooms.

The educational benefits of mixed-age grouping have been discussed by reformers from Montessori and Pestolozzi to Dewey. Since the 1930s, as educators have become increasingly aware of the limitations of a rigidly graded system, they have introduced more flexible organizational patterns. They have found that the nongraded organizational system recognizes and plans for a wide range of pupil abilities, provides for differential rates of progress, and adjusts to individual emotional and social needs.

A number of public and private schools that began as nongraded, emphasizing concern for individual continuous progress, have gradually changed to a multi-age vertical organization pattern. Increasing understanding of the developmental approach to education has resulted in renewed interest in Kentucky, Mississippi, and Oregon, where state legislators have mandated multi-age classes for grades K-3. A number of other states, including Pennsylvania, Florida, Alaska, Georgia, Claiforina, Texas, Tennessee, and New York, are reported to be developing similar programs.

From *Principal,* vol. 71, no. 5, p. 20–22, May 1992. Reprinted with permission.

DEFINING MIXED-AGE GROUPING

Mixed-age or multi-age groupings should not be confused with combination classes, in which two or more age groups are combined for administrative reasons, such as overcrowded conditions or small enrollments at one grade level (*see accompanying article* [in *Principal*, vol. 71, no. 5, May 1992]). Where combination classes mix ages out of necessity, multi-age groupings do it for perceived benefits.

Ironically, combination classes that began as a stopgap arrangement have become, in many instances, the preferred arrangement. Changes in teaching methods, concern for individual differences, and concern for the social needs of children have prompted some teachers of combination classes to see the long-term advantages of mixed-age groupings.

A rationale frequently proffered for mixed-age grouping is that a larger age span is more reflective of the child's society outside school, and that children are accustomed to associating with groups covering a wide age range. A related rationale is that such classes substitute for the children's experience within an "age-segregated society." Advocates of this view see multi-age grouping as a reaction to changes in family structure and a decrease in contact among age groups in other settings, such as nursery schools and day care centers.

A Choice of Groupings

For the past several years, Sidwell Friends Lower School has offered a single-age and a mixed-age option at each Pre-K–4 grade level, with no classroom spanning more than a two-year age range. At present, the mixed-age classes are PK-K, K-1, 1-2, 2-3, and two 3-4 classes. We find that a combination of vertical and same-age grouping allows us greater scope in meeting the needs of individuals and eliciting the greatest contribution from each student.

This combination of groupings also gives us a greater number of placement options each year. We have thirteen classrooms, and if all were single-age classrooms, we'd have thirteen placement choices. Because of mixed-age grouping, however, we have 19 options every year—an increase of almost 50 percent.

FOUR MISCONCEPTIONS

At Sidwell Friends, we have had to deal with several misconceptions about multi-age grouping. One is that multi-age vertical groups are less structured than single-grade horizontal ones. In my view, the tightness of structure in a classroom depends more on the style of teaching and organization than on the nature of the grouping.

Assuming that there is the same teacher-student ratio in both types of classes, and there are equal opportunities for individual attention and challenging learning experiences, the most important factor in determining if a child should be in a vertical or horizontal classroom is the fit of the teacher's teaching style and the student's learning style.

A second misconception is that mixed-age classrooms are meant to equalize children of different ages and abilities. In fact, vertical grouping offers children with a wide range of abilities and rates of progress a chance to work together. We do not track children by ability or age. We do not, for example, place "weak" or younger second graders with first graders, and "strong" or older second graders with third graders.

A third misconception is that the younger child in a mixed-age class will be "stretched" more than in a single-age class. Parents arguing in favor of this view incorrectly employ a sports metaphor: "I like to play tennis with someone just a little better than I am. It keeps me on my toes and improves my game." My response is: "How would you like to lose every game by just a little bit for the next five years, no matter how much you improve?"

> When older children "teach" newly learned skills to younger classmates, they strengthen their own understanding of these skills.

Older children are as academically challenged in the top half of a mixed-age class as they would be in a single-age class when there is an equally demanding curriculum and individual attention to learning style and academic level. Additionally, when older children "teach" newly learned skills to younger classmates, they strengthen their own understanding of these skills.

The last misconception is that, once children begin a mixed-age class in the younger of two grades, they must stay with the class for the second year. At Sidwell Friends, we follow our regular placement procedure at the end of each year, with teachers from adjacent grades discussing each child and determining the most suitable placement for the following year. Such factors as individual student needs, interests, temperament and learning styles are balanced with logistics that make for a cohesive class. As a result, some children in the lower age span of a mixed-age class may move into single-age classes, while some in horizontal groupings may be placed in the upper age span of a vertical group.

THE PROS OF MIXED-AGE GROUPING

Many of the studies done in the last thirty years have been supportive of mixed-age grouping. In their 1990 study of the subject, Katz, Evangelou, and Hartman found that:

1. The wide range of competencies in a mixed-age group provides students with opportunities to develop relationships and friendships with others who match, complement, or supplement their own needs and styles. Children in vertical groupings have a wide selection of models from whom they can learn—some older, some younger, some the same age. Mixed-age grouping provides older children with leadership opportunities and younger children with opportunities for more complex pretend play than they could initiate themselves.

2. Although some parents express concern about the likelihood of competition in a multi-age group, research indicates the opposite—that greater cooperation is often the result. And because such grouping appears to minimize competitive pressure, discipline problems that seem inherent in competitive environments are often substantially reduced.

3. Since most young children are not equally mature in areas of development at a given time, mixed-age grouping can be an effective strategy for dealing with their different rates of development. This grouping can be very helpful for children functioning below age-group norms in some developmental areas.

4. As a child interacts with children at different levels of cognitive maturity, intellectual growth is stimulated. Some pro-

ponents of mixed-age classes argue that the cognitive conflict likely to arise in mixed-age interaction provides situations for significant learning for younger children as they strive to accommodate to the more advanced understanding of their classmates.

"Give It a Try"

Imagine my excitement when I discovered an article ("Dual-Age Classroom: Questions and Answers" by Kay D. Woelfel) in the January 1992 issue of *Principal* addressing multi-age classes! We had started five such classes last fall after much discussion with parents and the central office, and I hoped the article would help our evaluation committee in assessing them.

I was wrong. The article described combination classes established to help balance student/teacher ratios in overcrowded "grade-levels." But multi-age classes have little in common with combined classes.

Combination classes are usually made up of top students from two grade levels, half of whom can work independently while the teacher works with the other half. The teacher develops two different sets of lesson plans for most subjects. In a multi-aged class, by contrast, heterogeneous children of two or more age groups are taught by the teacher who uses one set of lesson plans and employs varied strategies to group students at their appropriate levels of development and readiness.

We established multi-aged classes in our school to address the belief that children develop cognitively at differing rates, just as they do physically. After reading all the literature, we decided the jury was still out on whether multi-age configurations increase academic achievement as measured on standardized tests. Students' emotional and social growth seemed to be the areas most positively affected.

But emotional and social issues can block academic achievement, and we were intrigued with the idea that in multi-age classes students and teachers tend to lose track of grade levels and begin to see class members as unique individuals.

So far, we are pleased with the new configurations of our five classes. The teachers are challenged to make lessons meaningful and appropriate for everyone, and the children work cooperatively in a safe, comfortable setting. Although parents of some second graders were initially concerned that their children would not be challenged while they "waited" for the first graders to catch up, those fears have been removed.

I hope that our success with multi-age classes will encourage other schools to give it a try. These classes are a good option for children who need to work and learn in settings that more realistically mirror the real world.

Sue Bernheisel, Principal
Andrew J. Mitchell Primary School
Boulder City, Nevada

Other studies have determined that:

• Vertical grouping means that many children can have the same teacher or teaching team for more than one year, enabling teachers to use the knowledge they have gained about a child during the first year to plan learning experiences for the next year. Mixed-age grouping minimizes the get-acquainted time at the beginning of the year and provides children with strong continuity.

• In mixed-age groups, teachers' tendencies to teach all children the same lessons at the same time are reduced. Mixed-age grouping compels educators to organize learning activities and curriculum so that individuals and small groups of children can work on different tasks together.

THE CONS OF MIXED-AGE GROUPING

There are, of course, some disadvantages to mixed-age grouping that have been mentioned in research or personally observed:

1. When the number of children in a mixed-age classroom is small, it may be difficult for same-age, same-sex children to develop friendships. This problem can be lessened by encouraging cross-age friendships and by providing opportunities for same-age children in different classes to come together at recess, snack time, lunch, or for joint projects.

2. There can be a tendency for teachers of mixed-age groups to provide fewer challenges for older children. Sometimes it's easier for a teacher to step back and let an older child help the younger ones. Teachers must make an effort to consistently provide enriching experiences for older children in mixed-age classes.

3. Some younger children, especially if very competitive, may be frustrated by the perceived gap between their work and that of older students.

4. A mixed-age class may encounter more difficulty in scheduling items for individual students to work with special teachers.

5. Teachers must do more work in planning instruction for a wide age range of students.

In the final analysis, putting children of different ages together in the same space does not necessarily bring about either beneficial or negative experiences. The external organizational method of single-grade or mixed-age grouping is less significant in influencing the relationships among children and their learning than the quality of the classroom environment.

As a K-1 teacher in a Vermont school put it, "The less we expect kids to be the same, the more they will accept and enjoy the differences among them. When that type of atmosphere is achieved, kids are free to learn from each other, and teachers have more time to teach."

REFERENCES

Harkins, J. *Vertical Grouping Ten Years Later.* Germantown, Pa.: Germantown Friends School, 1977.

Katz, L. G.; Evangelou, D.; and Hartman, J. A. *The Case for Mixed-Age Grouping in Early Education.* Washington, D.C.: National Association for the Education of Young Children, 1990.

Lodish, R. *"Cross-Age Relationships in an After-School Center: An Observational Study of Children's Interactions With and Perceptions of Different Age Groups."* Ph.D. diss., Harvard University, 1976.

Mitchell, J. "Two Grades Are Better Than One." *Teacher,* April 1991.

On the Merits of Multiage Classrooms

by David Pratt, Ph.D.

This paper brings together evidence from a variety of fields which throws light on the practice of age segregation in schools. Strict age segregation is essentially a phenomenon of the last century. Research studies show no consistent benefits to age segregation, and some affective and social advantages from multiage grouping. It is concluded that multiage and multigrade classrooms are socially and psychologically healthy environments.

A PERENNIAL DEBATE

Reflection on the quality of learning environments is a hallmark of the educational professional. Those professionals who work in small schools often wonder about the costs and benefits of the multiage and multigrade classrooms with which they are more familiar than their colleagues in larger schools. This interest is currently shared by the increasing number of teachers in medium-sized schools who find themselves teaching split grades. Proposals to close small schools often act as a catalyst for debate on this issue, with the intuition of parents and teachers frequently pitted against the efficiency rationale of district administrators. Such debates usually end with the execution or reprieve of the school in question, but with the educational issue unresolved.

In this paper, I shall attempt to summarize evidence that bears on the question of the merits of multiage classrooms. This includes not only the findings of experimental research, but also relevant evidence from ethology, anthropology, and history. The weight of this evidence strongly suggests that multiage classrooms have many benefits to children which cannot be as fully realized in age-segregated classrooms.

From *Research in Rural Education*, vol. 3, no. 3, p. 111–115, 1986. Reprinted with permission.

THE HISTORICAL CONTEXT OF AGE SEGREGATION

Most of us grew up in an age-segregated school system. So did our parents and grandparents, and this makes it easy to assume that such a school structure is both natural and universal. In fact, it is universal neither geographically nor historically. A quarter of Scotland's primary schools have fewer than fifty students; 80% of Portuguese children go to schools with no more than two classrooms; and there are 11,000 one-teacher rural schools in France [34]. Age segregation, as practised in most large schools, is a relatively recent phenomenon, and one which runs counter to the pattern of upbringing of the young which previously existed for millions of years.

> Age segregation, as practised in most large schools, is a relatively recent phenomenon.

Studies of primates show that almost all of the 193 living species of monkeys and apes grow up in societies characterized by diversity of age. According to Jolly [26], "the striking characteristic of young, socially living primates is their social play" (p. 261). The context in which the young primate moves from dependence on the mother to adulthood is the mixed-age play group, whose members range from infancy to adolescence. In the play group, the young primate learns social and gender roles, control of aggression, and survival and nurturing skills. In general, the higher the primate is on the evolutionary scale, the more heterogeneous is the age composition of the play group.

A very similar pattern is found in anthropological studies of the approximately 180 hunting/gathering societies which survived into the present century, such as the Inuit, the Australian aborigines, and the !Kung San people of the Kalahari desert. Such societies typically live in groups of 30 to 40. Births are spaced a minimum of three years apart, so that the mother never has more than one infant to care for. The infant joins the play group after about the age of 18 months, imitating and relying on older children, who take responsibility for younger ones. Draper [13] records that "a typical gang of children joined temporarily in some play in the village might include a 5-year old boy, an 11-year-old girl, a 14-year-old boy, and a 2-year-old toddler hanging on the fringe of the action" (p. 202). Cross-cultural studies show that in simpler societies, children spend more time caretaking infants, and are more nurturant than in more complex cultures. In all societies, aggression is more frequent among age-mates than in mixed-age groups [50]. Konner [27] draws the following conclusions from the ethological and anthropological evidence:

> Infants are inept in relating to one another for the simple reason that they were never called on to do so during millions of years of evolution; consequently they could not have been selected for an ability to do this. They were selected instead for an ability to become integrated into a multiage group . . . The apes and protohominids went to considerable trouble to evolve for us a successful childhood in nonpeer play groups. Perhaps we should be a bit more cautious before we abandon the nonpeer pattern. (pp. 122-123)

The age-stratified culture in which we live is largely a product of the last two hundred years. In medieval Europe and in colonial America, children grew up surrounded by other children and adults of all different ages. Families were larger, and infant mortality and a high fertility rate resulted in a wide variance in sibling age. Schools and classrooms contained considerable age diversity. In the dedicated one-room school building that emerged in the eighteenth century, a full-time teacher would use individual and tutorial methods to instruct a group of 10 to 30 pupils ranging in age from 6 to 14 years [10].

The death-knell of the one-room school was sounded when Horace Mann [33], Secretary of the Massachusetts Board of Education, visited schools in Prussia in 1843 and reported that

> the first element of superiority in a Prussian school . . . consists in the proper classification of the scholars. In all places where the numbers are sufficiently large to allow it, the children are divided according to ages and attainments, and a single teacher has the charge only of a single class . . . There is no obstacle whatever . . . to the introduction at once of this mode of dividing and classifying scholars in all our large towns. (p. 84)

Within a decade, Mann's ideas were being widely accepted by administrators who saw in them a parallel with successful manufacturing practice [32]:

> The principle of the division of labor holds good in schools, as in mechanical industry. One might as justly demand that all operations of carding, spinning and weaving be carried out in the same room, and by the same hands, as insist that children of different ages and attainments should go to the same school and be instructed by the same teacher.

Legislation followed standardizing age of entry and establishing sequential grade levels and curricula. Population concentration and improved transportation facilitated the development of large schools. The death of the one-room school in the United States and Canada was delayed by the Depression, the world wars, and the long struggle of rural communities to preserve it against the will of urban educational bureaucracies [8]. But by the 1950s, the standard environment of youth was the suburb, consisting largely of middle-aged parents and school-age children. By then, the "generation gap" was accepted as a fact of life, and the over-60s, perceived as socially and economically marginal, were segregated in high-rise apartments, retirement villages, and homes for the elderly.

By the mid-twentieth century, classrooms were more narrowly segregated by age than ever before. In 1918 the standard deviation of age in American Grade 9 classrooms was 14.1 months; in 1952 it was 8.6 months [29]. Ability grouping, which became popular after about 1920, further reduced the variety present in classrooms. It was not until 1959 that the first major challenge to age segregation in schools appeared, in the form of *The Nongraded School* by Goodlad and Anderson. In the 1963 edition [19], the authors documented the variability in the intellectual, emotional, and physical growth of children and adolescents:

> Grouping children "homogeneously" on the basis of a single criterion does not produce a group that is homogeneous to the same degree judged by other criteria . . . Teachers who proceed as though their class of gifted and retarded pupils were homogeneous are fooling themselves and cheating their pupils. (p. 17)

The influence of the book was rapid. Within a few years, thousands of school districts were claiming that at least some of their schools were nongraded. But the movement turned out to be an archetypal case of fashionable rhetoric concealing educational inertia. The research on nongrading, which includes at least 50 doctoral theses, shows that although formal grade distinctions were often removed, the narrow age structure of classrooms usually remained intact. Goodlad [18] expressed his own disillusion in 1968:

> My own view . . . is that there are, indeed, precious few non-graded schools . . . The concepts guiding nongrading are becoming part of the rambling rhetoric, the cant of current educational orthodoxy. (p. 4)

The nongraded school movement was not powerful enough to overcome organizational structures which were politically safe and administratively convenient. But one thing it did was to stimulate a great deal of empirical research into the effects of multiage and multigrade grouping. The body of this research points to some significant benefits to pupils who are placed in multiage settings.

CHILDREN'S FRIENDSHIPS
Children's friendships, both in classrooms and in naturalistic settings, have been one theme of the multiage research. The general picture that emerges from these studies is one of increased competition and aggression within same-age groups and increased harmony and nurturance within multiage groups [24; 48]. When children and adolescents find themselves in a mixed-age context, they associate and make friends across a relatively wide age range [43]. Rhoades [42] found that children in a nongraded elementary school chose friends from two years older to two years younger than themselves. In a study of adolescents outside school in Salt Lake City [15; 37], it was found that 31% of companions were other adolescents more than two years older or younger. Adolescent boys tended to associate with girls about 1 1/2 years younger. While the average age difference among friendship groups in school was only 6 months, outside of school it was 14 months.

In the increasing number of high schools which are enrolling adults in regular classes, such friendships can cross generations. A student in one such class commented, "I would love to participate in a mixed-age class again. It is great the way the different age groups can work with each other." [46, p. 7]. In a classroom containing adolescents and senior citizens, a senior says, "I get along beautifully with the young students. I'm enjoying it all, even the homework" [4]; while a 17-year-old states, "I'm learning a great deal about life and living from them . . . I've learned that old age can be a wonderful thing." [5] The majority of older adults surveyed by Daum and Getzel [11] and by Spouse [45] expressed a preference for programs that allowed interactions with people of all ages.

> Multiage grouping appears particularly beneficial to the younger members of the group.

It is a characteristic of young people that they imitate and (both literally and figuratively) look up to children or adolescents who are older [3; 30] or whom they believe to be older [40]. One of the effects of this is that children receive maximum verbal stimulation and develop new vocabulary most rapidly when grouped with children slightly older than themselves [12; 20; 31; 49). Studies of tutoring support these conclusions. Tutoring has a greater effect on the achievement of both tutor and tutee when the tutor is older than when both tutor and tutee are the same age [9]. This is consistent with Piagetian research which indicates that interaction between individuals at different levels of maturity will stimulate disequilibrium, equilibration, and cognitive growth in the less mature partner [6; 41]. For these reasons, multiage grouping appears particularly beneficial to the younger members of the group [23]. In conventional classrooms, younger members suffer a disproportionate incidence of failure and, even more alarmingly, of suicide [47]. In contrast to this, Milburn [35] noted that the youngest students in the multiage classrooms he studied consistently outperformed their peers in age-segregated classrooms.

Experimental studies in preschool settings confirm the positive effects of multiage grouping on social and emotional development. Hammack [21] found that three-, four-, and five-year-old children made more progress in self-concept in multiage than in single-age groups. Goldman [17] found three- and four-year-olds in mixed-age classes were more sociable than those in single-age classes. And in Israel, Bizman et al. [2] found that children in age-heterogeneous kindergartens were significantly more altruistic than children in age-homogeneous kindergartens.

It seems that, while age is a determinant of friendship, children and adolescents choose friends who are at an equivalent level in terms of development rather than chronological age [22]. In a multiage situation, children will more readily find friends at their own level. This is supported by evidence that fewer isolates are found in multiage than in age-segregated classrooms [1; 51]. Younger children are particularly helpful in reducing the isolation of socially withdrawn older children when assigned to them as playmates [16]. As childhood isolation is a significant predictor of later psychiatric disorder [14; 38], this must be counted a significant benefit of the multiage classroom.

EXPERIMENTAL STUDIES OF MULTIAGE CLASSROOMS

A major purpose of this review was to survey the results of the available experimental research in multiage grouping in classrooms. A total of thirty experimental studies were located, conducted between 1948 and 1983 in the United States and Canada. All examined the results of multiage grouping in elementary schools. All "multiage" classes contained a range of two or three years. Achievement variables were usually reading and mathematics scores on standardized tests. Social/emotional variables were commonly self-concept and attitude toward school. Many of the studies suffer from imperfect control of differences between teachers and schools which elected or rejected multiage grouping. Too few of the studies reported sufficiently complete statistical data to allow more than a counting procedure for summation of the results.

Studies were classified as "favoring conventional grouping," "inconclusive," or "favoring multiage grouping," on the basis of the expressed judgment of their authors, which in all cases appeared to be justified by their findings. Table 1 shows the results for all 30 studies. Table 2 shows the results from those studies which were conducted as doctoral theses. Doctoral theses are

TABLE 1
Empirical Studies in Multiage Grouping
(30 Studies)

	Academic Achievement	Social/Emotional Development
Studies favoring conventional grouping	5	0
Inconclusive studies	13	6
Studies favoring multiage grouping	10	9

TABLE 2
Empirical Studies in Multiage Grouping
(10 Doctoral Studies)

	Academic Achievement	Social/Emotional Development
Studies favoring conventional grouping	1	0
Inconclusive studies	5	4
Studies favoring multiage grouping	2	3

in general likely to be relatively rigorous in their design, and meta-analyses have found theses more likely to report inconclusive results [44].

The findings summarized in Tables 1 and 2 suggest that multiage grouping has no consistent effect on academic achievement. Multiage grouping does, however, tend to be associated with better self-concept and attitude toward school. None of the 30 studies found a consistent negative relationship in this area. Similarly, in the one study located of a nongraded secondary school, academic achievement was unaffected, but the drop-out rate was significantly lower in the non-graded school [7]. Teacher attitudes appear to be determined by experience: teachers were generally found to approve of the structure with which they had become familiar [36].

Collectively, the empirical studies indicate that multiage grouping has no consistent effect on academic achievement, but has a generally benign effect on social and emotional development.

DIVERSITY AND UNIFORMITY

District administrators often use two arguments to support the closing of small schools. One is that such schools are financially inefficient; another is that their multiage classrooms are educationally undesirable. The first argument is fallible; recent research [34] shows that financial savings from such closings are often illusory, as they are subsequently eaten up by costs of transporting students. The research reviewed in this paper indicates that the second argument is also ill-founded. Multiage classrooms appear to convey a number of benefits, and no disadvantages, to their pupils.

Age-segregated classrooms are particularly difficult for children whose development differs from the norm. In conventional schools, the child of exceptional intellectual gifts is sometimes allowed or encouraged to "skip" a grade, which, although usually successful [28], is socially problematic and a poor substitute for genuine acceleration. The child whose development is slower than the norm faces the unmitigated disaster of grade repetition [25]. Even the least radical multiage structure, the split-grade classroom, can deal much more flexibly with both faster and slower learners. Some jurisdictions are now beginning to take note of these factors. In Canada, the Province of Ontario recently proposed for discussion a policy of flexible entry, multiage integration, and continuous progress in the primary division [39].

The social environment of young people during their formative years is a matter of considerable importance to educators and to parents. Conventional structures, though sanctioned by a century of familiarity, must be questioned if they stimulate rivalry, aggression, and isolation, for no apparent advantage. Environments that include a range of ages must be considered if they promise greater cooperation, nurturance, and friendship, for no apparent cost. The evidence on multiage grouping appears to confirm the basic principle that diversity enriches and uniformity impoverishes.

Conventional schools and classrooms could reap some of the benefits of diversity by developing programs of cross-age tutoring, by encouraging adults and senior citizens to participate in schools as students and volunteers, by organizing extracurricular activities that cut across grade and age lines, and by welcoming rather than resisting split grades. In small schools and multiage classrooms, teachers live with the daily challenge of working in environments that depart from the general norm. The creativity and inventiveness required exacts a toll in time and energy. But such educators may take encouragement from the fact that the mass of evidence indicates that, for their pupils, these environments are socially and psychologically healthy places.

NOTES

1. Adams, J. J. Achievement and social adjustment of pupils in combination classes enrolling pupils of more than one grade level. *Journal of Educational Research*, 1953, *47*, 151-155.

2. Bizman, A., Yinon, Y., Mivitzari, E., & Shavit, R. Effects of the age structure of the kindergarten on altruistic behavior. *Journal of School Psychology*, 1978, *16*, 154-160.

3. Blythe, D. A., Hill, J. P., & Smyth, C. K. The influence of older adolescents on younger adolescents: Do grade-level arrangements make a difference in behaviors, attitudes, and experiences? *Journal of Early Adolescence*, 1981, *1*, 85-110.

4. Bowering, C. LC students, old people walk hand-in-hand down a two-way street. Kingston *Whig-Standard*, 28 November 1978, p. 14.

5. Bowering, C. The young and old "bridge the gap" at a Kingston school. Kingston *Whig-Standard*, 7 November 1978, p. 16.

6. Bunting, J. R. Egocentrism: The effects of social interactions through multi-age grouping. (Doctoral dissertation, State University of New York at Buffalo, 1974). *Dissertation Abstracts International*, 1965, *35*, 6356A.

7. Chalfant, L. S. A three-year comparative study between students in a graded and nongraded secondary school (Doctoral dissertation, Utah State University, 1972). *Dissertation Abstracts International*, 1973, *33* 3178A.

8.   Cochrane, J. *The one-room School in Canada*. Toronto: Fitzhenry and Whiteside, 1981

9.   Cohen, P. A., Kulik, J. A., & Kulik, C. C. Educational outcomes of tutoring: A meta-analysis of findings. *American Educational Research Journal*, 1982, *19*, 237-248.

10. Cremin, L. A. *The transformation of the school: Progressivism in American education 1867-1957*. New York: Vintage Books, 1961.

11. Daum, M., & Getzel, G. S. Preference for age-homogeneous versus age-heterogeneous social interaction. Paper presented at the annual meeting of the Gerontological Society, San Diego, November 1980. (ERIC Document Reproduction Service No. ED 200 854).

12. Day, B., & Hunt, G. H. Multiage classrooms: An analysis of verbal communication. *Elementary School Journal*, 1974, *75*, 458-464.

13. Draper, N. Social and economic constraints on child life among the !Kung. In R. B. Lee & I. De Vore (Eds.), *Kalahari hunter-gatherers: Studies of the !Kung San and their neighbors*. Cambridge, MA: Harvard University Press, 1976, pp. 199-217.

14. Duck, S. *Friends for life*. Brighton, U.K.: Harvester Press, 1983.

15. Ellis, S., Rogoff, B., & Cromer, C. C. Age segregation in children's social interactions. *Developmental Psychology*, 1981, *17*(4), 399-407.

16. Furman, W., Rahe, D. F., Hartup, W. W. Rehabilitation of socially withdrawn preschool children through mixed-age and same-age socialization. *Child Development*, 1979, *50*, 915-922.

17. Goldman, J. A. Social participation and preschool children in same- versus mixed-age groups. *Child Development*, 1981, *52*, 644-650.

18. Goodlad, J. I. Editorial: The non-graded school. In *National Elementary Principal, the Nongraded School*. Washington, DC: NEA, 1968, pp. 4-5.

19. Goodlad, J. I. & Anderson, R. H. *The nongraded elementary school* (Rev. ed.). New York: Harcourt, Brace, and World, 1963.

20. Graziano, W., French, D., Brownell, C. A., & Hartup, W. W. Peer interaction in same- and mixed-age triads in relation to chronological age and incentive condition. *Child Development*, 1976, *47*, 707-714.

21. Hammack, B.G. Self-concept: Evaluation of preschool children in single- and multi-age classroom settings (Doctoral dissertation, Texas Women's University, 1974). *Dissertation Abstracts International*, 1975, *35*, 6572-6573.

22. Hartup, W. W. Cross-age versus same-age peer interaction: Ethological and cross-cultural perspectives. In V. L. Allen (Ed.), *Children as teachers: Theory and research on tutoring*. New York: Academic Press, 1976, pp. 41-55.

23. Hartup, W. W. Developmental implications and interactions in same- and mixed-age situations. *Young Children*. March 1977, 4-13.

24. Hartup, W. W. The social worlds of childhood. *American Psychologist*, 1979, *34*, 944-950.

25. Holmes, C. T., & Matthews, K. M. The effects of nonpromotion on elementary and junior high school pupils: A meta-analysis. *Review of Educational Research*, 1984, *54*(2), 225-236.

26. Jolly, A. *The evolution of primate behavior.* New York: Macmillan, 1972.

27. Konner, M. Relations among infants and juveniles in comparative perspective. In M. Lewis & L. A. Rosenblum (Eds.), *Friendship and peer relations.* New York: Wiley, 1975, pp. 99-129.

28. Kulik, J., & Kulik, C.-L. C. Effects of accelerated instruction on students. *Review of Educational Research*, 1984, *54*, 409-425.

29. Lennon, R. T., & Mitchell, B. C. Trends in age-grade relationship: A 35-year review. *School Society*, 1955, *82*, 123-125.

30. Lewis, M., Young, G., Brooks, J., & Michaelson, L. The beginnings of friendship. In M. Lewis & L. A. Rosenblum (Eds.), *Friendship and peer relations.* New York: Wiley, 1975, pp. 27-66.

31. Lougee, M. D., Grueneich, R., & Hartup, W. W. Social interaction in same- and mixed-age dyads of preschool children. *Child Development*, 1977, *48*, 1353-1361.

32. *Lowell School Committee Report of 1852.* Cited in D. Bruck, The schools of Lowell, 1824-1861. A case study in the origins of modern public education in America. Unpublished doctoral dissertation, Harvard University, 1970.

33. Mann, H. Seventh report to the Massachusetts Board of Education, 1843. Cited in E. P. Cubberley, *Readings in public education in the United States.* Westport, CT: Greenwood Press, 1970, 287-288.

34. Marshall, D. G. Closing small schools: Or when is small too small? *Education Canada*, 1985, *25*(3), 10-16.

35. Milburn, D. A study of multi-age or family-grouped classrooms. *Phi Delta Kappan*, 1981, *62*, 513-514.

36. Moodie, A. G. *A survey of teachers' opinions regarding multi-age classes.* Vancouver: Board of School Trustees, Department of Planning and Evaluation, 1971.

37. Montemayor, R., & Van Komen, R. Age segregation of adolescents in and out of school. *Journal of Youth and Adolescence*, 1980, *9*, 371-381.

38. Oden, S. A child's social isolation: Origins, prevention, intervention. In G. Cartledge & J. F. Milburn (Eds.), *Teaching social skills to children: Innovative approaches.* New York: Pergamon Press, 1980, pp. 179-202.

39. Ontario Ministry of Education. *Report of the early primary education project.* Toronto: Ontario Ministry of Education, 1985.

40. Peifer, M. R. *The effects of varying age-grade status of models on the imitative behavior of six-year-old boys.* Newark, DE: The University of Delaware, 1971.

41. Piaget, J. *The psychology of intelligence.* London: Routledge & Kegan Paul, 1950.

42. Rhoades, W. M. Erasing grade lines. *The Elementary School Journal,* 1966, *67*, 140-145.

43. Roopnarine, J. L., & Johnson, J. E. Socialization in a mixed-age experimental program. *Developmental Psychology,* 1984, *20*(5), 828-832.

44. Smith, M. L. Publication bias and meta-analysis. *Evaluation in Education: An International Review Series,* 1980, *4*(1), 22-24.

45. Spouse, B. M. *Participation motivation of older adult learners.* Paper presented at the annual meeting of the Association for Gerontology in Higher Education, Cincinnati, March 1981. (ERIC Document Reproduction Service No. ED 199 404).

46. Steurer, S. J. Findings about mixed-age learning. Paper presented at the annual meeting of the American Educational Research Association, Toronto, March 1978.

47. Uphoff, J. K., & Gilmore, J. Pupil age at school entrance: How many are ready for success? *Educational Leadership,* 1985, *43* (Sept.), 86-90.

48. Wakefield, A. P. Multi-age grouping in day care. *Children Today,* 1979, May-June, 26-28.

49. Way, J. W. Verbal interaction in multiage classrooms. *Elementary School Journal,* 1979, *79*(3), 178-186.

50. Whiting, B. B., & Whiting, J. W. M. *Children of six cultures: A psychocultural analysis.* Cambridge, MA: Harvard University Press, 1975.

51. Zerby, J. R. A comparison of academic achievement and social adjustment of primary school children in the graded and ungraded school programs (Doctoral dissertation, Penn State University, 1960). *Dissertation Abstracts International,* 1961, *21*, 2644.

A Study of Multi-Age or Family-Grouped Classrooms

by Dennis Milburn

This experiment in multi-age grouping revealed little difference in basic skills achievement levels but a big difference in attitudes toward school.

Deliberate mixing of age and grade levels in the elementary classroom has been common—even fashionable at times—over the past thirty years. A number of different terms describe this practice: family grouping, split level, mixed grade, etc. In each, however, a child remains in the same class with the same teacher for a number of years, most commonly three.

Multi-age grouping can start at any age. As new children enter a given group at the young end of the age range, older youngsters graduate. A typical pattern looks like this:

	Age Groups		
First year	A	B	C
Second year	X	A	B
Third year	Y	X	A

The rationale for multi-age grouping, by contrast, assumes cognitive benefits for children. We know, for example, that chronological age and mental age do not always correspond. Moreover, a child may excel in one curricular area and simultaneously experience difficulty in another. Such individual differences are the norm, but traditional grouping by specific age or grade level makes them hard to handle. The sequential, lock-step curriculum does not readily allow for flexible adjustments to individual needs.

From *Phi Delta Kappan*, vol. 62, no. 7, p. 513–514, March 1981. Reprinted with permission.

Multi-age grouping, by contrast, enables youngsters to work at different developmental levels without obvious remediation or "going back"— a situation that can cause emotional, social, or intellectual damage—and without special arrangements for acceleration. Curricular content can be matched to individual abilities, and youngsters have more time to assimilate and consolidate learnings in a familiar environment. A teacher who works with the same group for two or more years is also in a better position to evaluate each youngster's cognitive progress and to prevent fragmentation or unnecessary repetition of instruction.

Advocates also assume that multi-age grouping affords affective benefits. Cooperation among age groups is fostered. Age and achievement differences are taken into account and accepted by the group. Children observe the teacher relating to youngsters of different ages. They also avoid the trauma—for some, at least—of adjusting each year to a new adult with a different teaching style and unfamiliar expectations.

> A teacher who works with the same group for two or more years is also in a better position to evaluate each youngster's cognitive progress.

These are the presumed advantages of multi-age grouping. But what do children actually gain from placement in a multi-age classroom? To answer this question, I studied two schools of similar size (enrollments of approximately 350 each) over a five-year period. The experimental school had five multi-age classes with an average of twenty-five youngsters in each. One class of children ranged in age from six to eight, one from seven to nine, one from eight to ten, and two from nine to eleven. The control school assigned all youngsters to specific, sequential grade levels and emphasized an orderly progression in curricular content. The two schools were located in similar socioeconomic areas in the inner suburbs of two cities approximately thirty miles apart (Greater Vancouver and Victoria, British Columbia). Neither school had major problems of any kind. Both had cooperative parent associations. The staff members in the two schools seemed relaxed, and both schools were pleasant places to visit.

I used four tests to compare youngsters in these two schools: the Gates-MacGinitie Reading Test, the California

Achievement Test in Mathematical Computation, the Piers-Harris Children's Self-Concept Scale, and the National Foundation for Educational Research (NFER) Attitude Survey. Any test administered to a specific grade level in the control school was also given to a similar number of age-mates in the experimental school. All tests were administered and scored by independent researchers; classroom teachers were not involved in the testing procedure.

I found little difference in basic skills achievement levels between youngsters in multi-age and traditional grade-level groups. Multi-age classes did score significantly higher on the vocabulary section of the reading test, however. One of two factors may account for this finding. First, teachers in multi-age classrooms may have placed greater emphasis on oral language and on verbal exchange of ideas. A second possibility is that teachers working in multi-age settings tend to speak at a level geared to the comprehension abilities of the older children; such modeling could conceivably boost the vocabulary maturity of younger children in the group.

> Multi-age classes did score significantly higher on the vocabulary section of the reading test.

The performance of the youngest age group in each multi-age class is of particular interest. In all cases these children scored higher on the basic skills tests than did age-mates in the control school. The oldest children in multi-age groups, by contrast, performed much like their counterparts in the control school. The seeming advantage of multi-age grouping for younger children may stem from emulation; perhaps younger children in such groups strive to attain the academic levels they actually see the older children achieving.

Children of all ages in the experimental school also had a more positive attitude toward school than did their counterparts in traditional grade-level groups (see Table 1). Data from the NFER Attitude Survey support this finding. Sixty-one percent of children in multi-age groups disagreed or strongly disagreed with the statement, "I dislike schoolwork," for example, compared with 9% of youngsters in the control school. Twenty percent of multi-age grouped youngsters agreed or strongly agreed that they disliked schoolwork, compared with 81% of children who were grouped by grade level. Similar differences

Table 1. Comparative Mean Scores on the Piers-Harris Self-Concept Scale

	Sex	Multi-Age Groups Mean	Grade-Level Groups Mean	Variance
Grade 1/Age 6	M	60	44	16
	F	78	57	21
Grade 2/Age 7	M	92	76	16
	F	94	74	20
Grade 3/Age 8	M	77	72	5
	F	71	68	3
Grade 4/Age 9	M	85	71	14
	F	91	81	10
Grade 5/Age 10	M	87	79	8
	F	72	70	2
Grade 6/Age 11	M	89	81	8
	F	78	70	8

between experimental and control groups showed up on the statement, "I think school is boring." Forty-six percent of children in multi-age classes strongly disagreed, compared with 2% of youngsters in grade-level groups. On the other hand, 68% of students in grade-level groups strongly agreed that school is boring, compared with only 8% of children in multi-age classes. It is difficult to discount the teacher/student relationship as a variable when one attempts to explain these differences.

For teachers working with multi-age groups, selective use of traditional curricular content becomes essential. (It is impossible to teach three complete grade-level curricula within the time constraints of the school year.) This selective approach to curriculum apparently does not reduce student achievement, however. One unanswered question is whether teachers need special training to teach multi-age groups effectively. During the five years of my study, some teachers in the experimental school grew visibly more comfortable with and more competent at teaching a variety of age groups simultaneously. Others tried multi-age classes for a year and chose to return to traditional grade-level grouping patterns.

The findings of this study suggest that multi-age classes may be of special benefit to slow learners. Such children may profit from the tendency to emulate older youngsters. Such children also can take time to assimilate learning in a familiar classroom environment with a familiar teacher. Time is on the side of the children in multi-age classes. But I do not mean to suggest that multi-age classes are suitable only for slow learners.

Although multi-age grouping promises no significant gains in basic skills, it does seem to engender positive attitudes toward school. Perhaps the safest conclusion is this: Multi-age grouping is simply one of a number of strategies for teaching youngsters. It is neither the "ideal" method nor is it a panacea for all educational ills.

The Benefits of Nongraded Schools

by Barbara Nelson Pavan

Educators and parents looking to implement a nongraded program can draw on 25 years of research supporting the success of such school organization.

The 1960s and 1970s were a time of high interest in nongraded schooling. The educational press carried a number of articles on the topic, and many research studies were conducted. John Goodlad and Robert Anderson's revision of *The Nongraded Elementary School* (1963) provided the rationale for schools attempting nongraded programs.

That book was revised again in 1987, marking a new period of interest in nongraded schooling. Kentucky and Oregon now mandate nongraded/continuous-progress primary units as vehicles for school improvement, and other state departments of education and school districts are considering the implementation of nongraded programs. This renewed attention presents an opportune time to review research that has compared the effectiveness of graded and nongraded schools.

DEFINING NONGRADED

A nongraded school does not use grade-level designations for students or classes. Progress is reported in terms of tasks completed and the manner of learning, not by grades or rating systems. A team of teachers generally works with a team of students who are regrouped frequently according to the particular task or activity and student needs or interests. Many times these are multiage heterogeneous groups pursuing complex problem-solving activities in interdisciplinary thematic units.

From *Educational Leadership*, vol. 50, no. 2, p. 22–25, 1992. Reprinted with permission.

Students are active participants in their learning and in the collection of documentation to be used for assessment and evaluation. The continuous progress of pupils is reflected in students' growth of knowledge, skills, and understanding, not movement through a predetermined sequence of curriculum levels.

THIS REVIEW

We considered studies published after 1967 for this review because it seemed most likely those researchers would have had access to a sufficient knowledge base on nongraded education. Nine descriptors were used to search for the studies: nongraded, nongradedness, nongrading, continuous progress, multiunit, individually guided education, multiage, ungraded, and mixed age.

To be included in this review, students in graded and nongraded schools with similar populations had to be compared using standardized test measures, or nongraded students had to be tested before and after the implementation of a nongraded program. We accepted for analysis elementary school studies conducted in the United States and Canada for at least one academic year. The studies included all subject areas and had to cover more than one classroom.

Sixty-four research studies published between January 1968 and December 1990 met these criteria. A number of the studies had been conducted in individually guided education (IGE) programs or in open space buildings, or they were referred to as team teaching. This review of nongraded education was narrowed to three specific topics: academic achievement, mental health indicators, and achievement for a variety of at-risk populations.[1]

ACADEMIC ACHIEVEMENT

Standardized academic achievement tests were used in 57 of the studies. Of those studies, 52 (91 percent) indicated that for all comparisons, the nongraded groups performed better (58 percent) or as well as (33 percent) the graded groups on measures of academic achievement. In only 9 percent of the studies did the nongraded students do worse than the graded students.

It seems rather remarkable that pupils in nongraded schools scored so well. Nongraded schools respond to individual differences by adjusting curriculum and thus may not cover what traditional textbooks do. As such, nongraded students may not be exposed to all the material that graded students cover. Yet nongraded students overwhelmingly performed as well as or better than graded students on achievement tests emphasizing mastery of content that is generally not the primary focus of the nongraded school.

MENTAL HEALTH

We included a mental health component in 42 of the studies. These measures presented data on school anxiety and other attitudes toward school, self-esteem, and self-concept. While the results on school anxiety were unclear, pupils in nongraded schools had more positive attitudes than those in graded schools, although they were likely to laugh more and less likely to raise their hands to get permission to speak. Students in nongraded schools scored higher than graded students on the Coopersmith Self-Esteem Inventory, except in one study with no significant differences. The same pattern was noted in studies that used the Piers Harris Children's Self-Concept Scale.

> Nongraded schools respond to individual differences by adjusting curriculum and thus may not cover what traditional textbooks do.

Overall on mental health and school attitudes, 52 percent of the studies indicated nongraded schools were better for students. Forty-three percent found that nongraded and graded schools had a similar influence on students. Only 5 percent found nongraded worse than graded schools. Students in nongraded schools were more likely to have positive self-concepts, high self-esteem, and good attitudes toward school than students in graded schools.

LONGITUDINAL STUDIES

While most of the research studies reported data from one year, 17 presented data over a number of years. In those studies, students completing nongraded primary programs had higher academic achievement than those in graded schools. More pupils attending nongraded primary schools started 4th grade with their entering class than did children from traditional grade-designated classrooms. This happens because there is no retention in a primary program. Students in nongraded intermediate programs had higher or similar academic achievement, more positive attitudes toward school, and similar self-esteem than those in graded programs.

Seven studies compared students who had spent their entire elementary school years in the same nongraded school with those who spent the same years in a traditional school. All those studies that reported academic achievement found superior performance by nongraded students. On mental health measures, students from nongraded settings felt more positive or

---

Research on Nongraded Programs

1. Research studies comparing nongraded and graded schools provide a consistent pattern favoring nongradedness.

2. The nongraded groups performed better (58 percent) or as well as (33 percent) the graded groups on measures of academic achievement.

3. On mental health and school attitudes, 52 percent of the studies indicated nongraded schools as better for students, 43 percent similar. Only 5 percent showed nongraded as worse than graded schools.

4. The benefits of students of nongradedness increase as students have longer nongraded experiences.

5. Blacks, boys, low socioeconomic level students, and underachievers benefit from a nongraded program.

---

the same as graded students. After five years in one nongraded, open space program, significantly fewer nongraded students were referred for discipline in junior high school.

AT-RISK STUDENTS

In 18 of the research reports we analyzed, data were analyzed for various populations: black students; underachievers; students of low socioeconomic status: and boys, who seem to experience more difficulty in the early years of learning and are often considered at risk.

With the exception of one study, boys in nongraded schools scored better on achievement tests than boys in graded schools. While boys in nongraded schools generally had better attitudes toward self and school, one of five mental health measures in a Canadian study indicated boys in nongraded settings had a poorer attitude toward school than graded boys.

Except for one study in which the multigrade students received only individualized instruction, blacks in nongraded schools had higher academic achievement than those in graded schools. In all comparative studies with data on black students, those in nongraded schools had better self-concepts and more positive attitudes toward school, teachers, and learning than those in graded schools.

> Underachievers in nongraded schools had better self-concepts, attitudes toward school, and academic achievement.

Underachievers in nongraded schools had better self-concepts, attitudes toward school, and academic achievement than underachievers in graded schools. Students of lower socioeconomic status also showed greater academic achievement when placed in nongraded schools.

NONGRADED IMPLEMENTATION

Only five studies of schools with individually guided education used an instrument to assess the implementation of nongraded practices. In those studies that looked at a wide variation in implementation, students in schools with high implementation of nongradedness had higher academic achievement, more positive attitudes toward school, and better self-concepts than those in schools with low implementation.

A 1971 study used responses to a teacher questionnaire to develop a nongraded index. Academic achievement was significantly higher in the school that showed the most characteristics of nongraded education than in the least nongraded school. In a 1973 study, program descriptions for six schools were assessed on a nongraded scale. Students in a strong nongraded program had more positive attitudes toward school and better self-concepts. The results showed higher academic achievement for both average and below average learners.

Guarino (1982) documented teaching practices using a modified version of an observational instrument developed by Pavan (1973) in order to locate two schools, one clearly nongraded and one clearly graded. Using students matched for age, sex and IQ, he found that students in the nongraded school had higher academic achievement, lower anxiety, and higher self-concepts than those in the graded school. Of all of the studies that looked at implementation, this one provides the best evidence in support of nongradedness.

SUMMARY

The 64 research studies cited in this review clearly support the use of nongraded/continuous-progress programs. Students in nongraded settings do as well as or better than students in traditional self-contained classes in terms of both academic achievement and mental health. We find these results despite the fact that the instruments used were standardized in traditionally structured schools. Given this strong evidence, parents and educators can be assured that students will flourish in a nongraded school.

NOTE

1.   All reference for this review and a comprehensive table giving details of each study are available in Anderson and Pavan (1993).

REFERENCES

Anderson, R.H., and B.N. Pavan. (1993). *Nongradedness: Helping It to Happen*, Lancaster, Pa.: Technomic Press.

Goodlad, J.I., and R.H. Anderson, (1987). *The Nongraded Elementary School*, New York: Teachers College Press. Revised editions in 1959 and 1963 published by Harcourt Brace Jovanovich, New York.

Guarino, A.R. (1982). "An Investigation of Achievement, Self-Concept, and School Related Anxiety in Graded and Nongraded Elementary Schools." Doctoral diss., Rutgers University.

Pavan, B.N. (February 1973). "Nongradedness? One View," *Educational Leadership 30*, 5:401-403.

Pavan, B.N. (March 1973). "Good News: Research on the Nongraded Elementary School." *Elementary School Journal* 73:233-42.

Pavan, B.N. (1977). "The Nongraded Elementary School: Research on Academic Achievement and Mental Health." *Texas Tech Journal of Education* 4:91-107.

Response

The Nongraded Elementary School

Great Potential, But Keep It Simple

by Robert E. Slavin

At the 1992 American Educational Research Association meeting in San Francisco, Roberto Guitérrez and I presented a review of research on the achievement effects of the nongraded elementary school. In general, our findings were consistent with those of Barbara Pavan's review; we also found many more positive than negative effects. However, we compared effect sizes[1] for each study to characterize the strengths of the effects, and we broke the studies into four main categories according to program characteristics. We found very different effects according to these characteristics.

The most positive achievement effects were for the simpler forms of nongrading generally evaluated during the 1960s, early in the nongraded movement. We found a median effect size of +.46 for programs in which only one subject (almost always reading) was nongraded. These programs strongly resemble the Joplin Plan, cross-grade grouping for reading (see Slavin 1987). We also calculated a median effect size of +.34 for nongraded programs that incorporated multiple subjects but still primarily involved cross-grade grouping, not other elements.

In the 1970s, as nongraded programs became more complex, began to incorporate individualized instruction, and became more like open schools, the achievement effects began to be much smaller. For programs incorporating individualized instruction, we found a median effect size of essentially zero (+.02). Effects of individually guided education were only slightly more positive (ES=+.11).

From *Educational Leadership*, vol. 50, no. 2, p. 24, 1992. Reprinted with permission.

Our conclusions suggest that the effectiveness of non-graded elementary programs depends in large part on the features of the program, especially the degree to which nongrading is used as a grouping method rather than as a framework for individualized instruction.[2]

It is hard to know how relevant findings are to the conditions of today, when curriculum and instruction are changing rapidly. Yet at least they provide a cautionary note. There is no magic in nongradedness. Nongraded organization can contribute to instructional effectiveness, but the curriculum and instructional methods used within a nongraded framework are as important as the school organization plan in determining the ultimate effects.

NOTES

1. Proportion of a standard deviation by which experimental groups exceed control groups.

2. Copies of "Achievement Effects of the Nongraded Elementary School: A Retrospective Review" are available for $6.25 from the Center for Research on Effective Schooling for Disadvantaged Students, Johns Hopkins University, 3505 N. Charles St., Baltimore, MD 21218.

REFERENCES

Guitérrez, R., and R. E. Slavin. (April 1992). "Achievement Effects of Nongraded Elementary School: A Retrospective Review." Paper presented at the annual meeting of the American Educational Research Association, San Francisco.

Slavin, R. E. (Fall 1987). "Ability Grouping and Student Achievement in Elementary Schools: A Best-Evidence Synthesis." *Review of Educational Research 57*, 3: 293-336.

Reply

Nongradedness: Not Simply a Grouping Scheme

by Barbara Nelson Pavan

As Robert Slavin indicates in his response, we are in general agreement about the positive achievement effects of nongradedness. Additionally, my research looks at the generally positive effects on mental health measures and for various disadvantaged groups. Guitérrez and Slavin (1992) report some different effects after dividing the studies into four categories. Other category systems could easily be devised that would influence the results. Individually guided education might be divided into two categories: the Wisconsin program, which has a curriculum focus; and the Kettering Program, with the multiunit, teaming focus. The 1971 Engel and Cooper study, with an effect size of +1.10 and an index of nongradedness rarely found in this research, should have been included in the four categories rather than consigned to category five for studies lacking explicit descriptions of the nongraded program.

Researchers might debate the technical details of methods, but we remain in agreement that nongradedness generally produces positive results for children.

I agree with Slavin that the relevance of past research to the present is uncertain. Goodlad wrote in *The Nongraded Elementary School* (1987), "What I would stress now, far more than I did then, would be the philosophy behind nongradedness, and this must infuse much more than merely school structure" (p. xii). Nongradedness is not simply a grouping scheme but a philosophy that demands the provision of appropriate and rich educational experiences for each child.

From *Educational Leadership*, vol. 50, no. 2, p. 25, 1992. Reprinted with permission.

REFERENCES

Goodlad, J.I., and R. H. Anderson. (1987 rev. ed.). *The Nongraded Elementary School.* New York: Teachers College Press.

Guitérrez, R., and R. E. Slavin. (April 1992). "Achievement Effects of Nongraded Elementary School: A Retrospect Review." Paper presented at the annual meeting of the American Educational Research Association, San Francisco.

A Look at Multi-Age Classrooms

By Deborah L. Cohen

To proponents of ungraded or mixed-age classrooms, letting pupils develop at their own pace helps those at differing ability levels push and pull each other along. Programs built on such a philosophy shun the restriction of individual grade levels. They offer, instead, flexible groupings that encompass a two- or four-year span, allowing movement between levels for those pupils ready to advance or needing more help in a subject.

Many schools experimented with ungraded classes in the 1960s, often unsuccessfully. But the concept is drawing renewed attention today as a way of curbing ability tracking and grade retention, two factors a growing number of educators identify as the detrimental precursors to failure for some young children. Experts also see ungraded units as a way to steer schools away from competitive and overly academic instruction in the early grades and toward methods grounded in hands-on learning, play, and exploration.

> Experts also see ungraded units as a way to steer schools away from competitive and overly academic instruction in the early grades.

With school reform efforts focusing more and more on the importance of the early years, notes Vito Perrone, director of teacher education programs at Harvard University, there has been growing recognition of the "need to provide children with a very strong base . . . out of which they can move confidently" into the upper grades. "People are asking how to assure that the early years are not years of failure," says Perrone. One way, he suggests, is to "think about the pri-

From *The Education Digest*, vol. 55, p. 20–23, May 1990. Reprinted with permission.

mary years as a developmental period where some children will move more rapidly than others."

The National Association for the Education of Young Children (NAEYC) promoted that view in its 1987 guidelines on "developmentally appropriate practice," which have gained broad recognition in the field. Taking the concept a step further, the National Association of State Boards of Education issued a report last year calling for new primary school units to provide developmentally paced learning for 4- to 8-year-olds. The National Association of Elementary School Principals (NAESP) is expected to issue similar recommendations next year.

> **Ungraded classrooms date back to the "one-room school" that was the norm up until the nineteenth century.**

Ungraded classrooms, researchers point out, date back to the "one-room school" that was the norm up until the nineteenth century. As John I. Goodlad and Robert H. Anderson note in *The Nongraded Elementary School*, the current system of grouping pupils by grades developed partly in response to the public school movement demand for efficient ways to organize large numbers of children. They and other educators also cite the role of European instructional influences, teacher training schools, the textbook industry and standardized testing in institutionalizing a system predicated on mastery of specific items at specific grade levels.

SYSTEM FAILURES

Critics of the system have argued that it fails to accommodate wide variations in children's rates of learning, and have decried the use of "social promotion," retention, and grade skipping to place students who fall behind or move ahead of their grade-level peers. Most recently, educators and child psychologists have raised concern about the effects of rigid academic programs and early grade retention on young pupils, whose developmental patterns vary widely and who are particularly vulnerable to being stigmatized as slow learners. To eliminate the need for such practice, proponents of ungraded schools advocate a model that allows pupils to advance from one concept skill level to the next as they are ready, regardless of age or grade.

Goodlad and Anderson cite 1970s research showing that standardized achievement test comparisons "tend to favor" nongraded programs, and that pupils in those programs may have improved chances of good mental health and positive school attitudes. The ungraded model, they suggest, is "particularly beneficial" for minorities, boys, underachievers, and low-income pupils.

Comparisons of achievement in graded and nongraded programs are inconclusive, maintains Bruce A. Miller, a rural education specialist with the Northwest Regional Educational Laboratory and author of a new handbook for rural educators on multigrade classrooms. But data on attitudes and peer relations, he says, have "tended overwhelmingly to favor multi-age grouping."

Current hard data on that topic is limited, but advocates cite research highlighting the pitfalls of retention and the benefits of methods often used in multigrade settings. "When you combine the evidence from cross-age studies, mixed-ability grouping, and cooperative-learning literature, you've got a super case for mixed-age grouping," says Lilian G. Katz, director of the ERIC Clearinghouse on Elementary and Early Childhood Education at the University of Illinois.

FIRM ENTRENCHMENT

Despite scattered forays into open schooling, team teaching, and individually guided education—all approaches that tap elements of the continuous-progress model—graded schools remain firmly entrenched. In "The Multigrade Classroom: A Resource Handbook for Small, Rural Schools," Miller notes that multi-age grouping arrangements have played a powerful role in rural schools out of "economic and geographic necessity." But in educational mainstream, Goodlad and Anderson write, "nongrading never became a movement as such." Elements of the ungraded approach did become "driving forces in school organization" in the 1960s and 1970s, according to Miller, but most "efforts to recapture the ideal of the one-room school were unsuccessful."

The "ungraded primary units" being promoted today bear little resemblance to earlier ventures, and, in the view of many experts, may stand a better chance of success. Efforts at multi-age grouping stand a better chance now says Carolyn H. Cummings, a consultant for NAESP, because "we have considerably more information about how children learn."

"We're trying to reinitiate that process with a great deal more knowledge," adds Laura Mast, a consultant for the North Carolina Department of Education. Other experts warn, however, that several obstacles must be overcome for the "reinitiation" to succeed. The NAEYC has stopped short of promoting ungraded units, for example, depicting them as merely "one strategy to implement developmentally appropriate primary grades curricula," according to Susan Bredekamp, director of professional development for NAEYC. "You can still achieve an individualized curriculum" in graded classes, she says, "if there is good communication between teachers…and you don't have rigid expectations or promotions standards.

> **Ungraded methods generally require better organizational skills, more work, and more support from administrators.**

"We have to recognize the fact that not everybody is trained to work with multi-age grouping," she adds. "Teachers have been trained to think in terms of discrete grade structures," she suggests, and may not be prepared for major structural changes.

Studies on the effectiveness of multi-age grouping show, Miller says, that "the most critical variable is the skill of the teacher." Ungraded methods generally require better organizational skills, more work, and more support from administrators, he says.

Some also note that textbooks have foiled efforts to regroup children. Goodlad and Anderson have argued, for example, that texts keyed to grade levels "nurture conformity and tempt teachers to cover material whether or not it is appropriate to the wide range of individual differences among pupils."

The lack of curriculum materials for ungraded approaches "makes it really difficult for teachers who are inclined to do it and don't have the confidence to strike out on their own," says Harriet Egertson, administrator of the Nebraska Department of Education Office of Child Development. But, she adds, some materials for whole-language reading, manipulative math, and technology-based writing are suitable for a mixed-age approach.

But some experts question whether curriculum development has advanced enough to support multi-age grouping.

They also fear, Perrone notes, that the push for national goals and uniform testing programs could work against such reforms. Others argue that the ungraded approach itself is flawed.

Its backers have not, says James K. Uphoff, director of laboratory experiences at the College of Education and Human Services at Wright State University in Dayton, Ohio, "publicly acknowledged what the literature of the 1960s said about ungraded multi-age units—that 30 to 40 percent of children will take not four years, but five years, to get through grades K-3." William Thompson, executive director of communications for the Philadelphia school system, says that when that district tried continuous-progress models several years ago, officials found the reverse—that too many children were being "moved along" without adequate preparation. "We did not find that to work over time," Thompson says, "and we don't anticipate going back."

> Others say the growing diversity of the student population works to the advantage of the ungraded movement.

Proponents, however, are confident that one major drawback for earlier attempts at multi-age grouping—their misalignment with trends fostered by the reform movement—may be receding in importance. In the 1960s, Perrone notes, educators were exploring "real books and activity-oriented approaches" associated with developmental approaches, but the "back to basics" movement of the 1970s "undermined a lot of the interest." An increased emphasis on testing and the "push downward" of formal academics to earlier ages that continued in the 1980s also discouraged ungraded approaches.

Perrone, among others, points out that the reforms being promoted as schools move into the 1990s could be more hospitable to multi-age classrooms. Multi-age grouping also holds more promise now, Egertson argues, because it brings together practices at the forefront of current reform thinking, including team teaching, cooperative learning, literature-based reading, and reductions in "pull-out" programs for remedial and special-education students.

Others say the growing diversity of the student population works to the advantage of the ungraded movement. "The changing demographics, more than the philosophical arguments, will force us into a search for school practices designed to accommodate these individual differences without loss of educational quality in schools," conclude Goodlad and Anderson.

"The environment right now is probably more conducive than it has been for 15 years to developmental programs in the early years—and to an ungraded primary as one direction," Perrone concurs.

In Practice

Sixty years ago I knew everything; now I know nothing; education is a progressive discovery of our own ignorance.—Will Durant

The progressive discovery Durant speaks of is personal, yet that same concept seems to apply universally as experience helps one unravel the mysteries of education in its broadest sense. In fact, the essays in this section address that very issue: what we learn…"in practice," as opposed to (or in complement to) what we learn "in theory."

The opening piece by the DelForges offers helpful suggestions for combination classes. The article features teaching tips from K–8 teachers and ideas on the composition of groupings—factors considered are responsibility, academic ability, age, and social maturity. The authors propose ideas on integrating curricula, peer tutoring, planning, the use of centers and contracts, and assistants. To ensure success of the non-graded programs, suggestions for administrators are included.

In a second article, Gaustad discusses class composition, team teaching, classroom organization and materials, flexible grouping strategies, integrated curricula, assessment, and evaluation. This writing is so clear and succinct, it is an ideal, must-read selection for teachers involved in nongraded, multiage, continuous progress programs. The theme of balance permeates this pragmatic piece.

A comprehensive article prepared by Miller summarizes six key instructional dimensions that affect successful multigrade teaching. Among the factors are organization, management and discipline, curriculum, instructional delivery, self-directed learning, and peer tutoring. Another vote for experienced and skillful teachers is registered, the writer says, "the abilities and behaviors required of multigrade teachers may be different than those of a teacher in a traditional classroom, and the coordinating activities more difficult."

Finally, a collection of short pieces from an issue of the High Expectations newsletter focusing on the theme of multiage classrooms is included. The essays range from theoretical rationales to practical strategies for immediate classroom use. The strategies include a multiple intelligences approach to instruction, a writer's workshop model, methods for integrated studies, and ideas for recruiting parents as part of the team. Two real-life experiences in multiage groupings highlight this group of articles.

Grouping Students and Helpful Suggestions for Combination Classrooms

by Clarence DelForge, Linda DelForge, and Charles V. DelForge

The one room rural school generally had students from the first through the eighth grade in all one classroom. Although most of the one room schools are gone today we still have Combination Classrooms (CC) even in the large urban school districts. Often state laws create the CCs because of the mandated classroom size. When the law states a maximum classroom size, schools find that students wanting to come to school do not arrive in the required maximum sizes. They always have a few students over or under the classroom limit and this creates a CC.

The CC is defined as having two or more grade levels in one classroom. The selecting of students for CCs has always presented problems for principals, teachers and parents. Research has not addressed this problem properly over the years because CCs are the "back water" of education. Everyone recognizes there are problems with CCs but no one seems to really care about them. The major purpose of this paper was to ask CC teachers what they thought was the best way to select students for a CC. While asking about the best way to group, we asked the CC teachers to share some of their teaching tips or suggestions on how to teach a CC.

Most of the data for this article (184 responses) was collected from teachers at the yearly Combination Classroom Conference at Western Carolina University. Because of the concerns

From Linda Delforge, Clarence Delforge, and Charles Delforge (Report No. 018 596). Cullowhee, NC: *Elementary Education and Reading*, (ERIC Document Reproduction Service No. ED 343 749) p. 1–8, 1992. Reprinted with permission.

expressed at these conferences a questionnaire was sent to 100 CC teachers in 28 rural school districts of North Carolina. We had a 72% rate of return on our mailing which, combined with the questionnaires filled out at the CC conferences, yielded a grand total of 256 CC teachers who completed the questionnaire. K-8 teachers were asked the following questions:

1. What is the best way to select the students who are going to be placed in Combination Classrooms?

2. Would you please share with us some of your teaching tips or suggestions that you have found from teaching in a Combination Classroom.

3. Number of years of teaching

4. Number of years you have taught a CC

The strength of this study comes from the wide array of experiences of the CC teachers. There was a balance between the novice and the more experienced teachers. Table I points out the range of teaching experience: from one year to 30. The 1-10 years of experience was the largest sample and perhaps this was due to the fact that more of the least experienced teachers attended the Combination Classroom conference in search of additional help.

Table I
Years of Teaching Experience

1-10 years of experience 38%
11-20 years of experience 35%
21-30 years of experience 27%

From Table II we see that the average number of times the teachers had taught a CC ranged from 4 to 8 times. The data suggests that either CCs are more common than they were 20-30 years ago or else beginning teacher are more likely to be

Table II
Average Number of Times Teachers Taught
A Combination Classroom

Years of Experience	Number of Times Assigned to Teach a CC
1-10 years of experience	4
11-20 years of experience	6
21-30 years of experience	8

assigned a CC. Teachers with 10 years or less experience averaged four CCs, while those who had taught 11-20 years averaged six and 21-30 averaged only eight times. After ten years of teaching the average teacher had four CCs: it then took 20 years of teaching experience to have four more CCs.

One might assume that the more experienced teachers have either learned to say no or are not required to teach CC classrooms as often as the more inexperienced teachers. Administrators seem to always assign the least experienced teachers the most demanding teaching assignments, which is really not the most professional thing to do.

GROUPING FOR COMBINATION CLASSROOMS

The most often suggested way to group students for a CC (27%) was to group them by responsibility. Responsibility means that the students are independent workers and self-starters. The teachers felt that time was a big factor in teaching a CC. Having enough time to work with students in a regular classroom is difficult, but some teachers felt the problem of time management was compounded in a CC. If students are responsible workers they can be on their own and successfully handle their independent time. Students who are self-starters require less time for monitoring, which can free the teacher to work with others.

The second most frequent suggestion (20%) was to group students by academic ability. Teachers would put the bright students from each grade level together. The teachers felt that academically bright students would be easier to work with because they require less time to teach. Bright children catch on faster than slower students and require less repetition.

The third highest suggestion (15%) was to group the students by having the best disciplined students together. These teachers felt that even bright students can become behavior problems. Again the time factor came into play because the teachers did not want to spend instructional time disciplining students. Students who require disciplining cause the class to be off task and learning to stop.

The next highest suggestion (14%) was to group high academically achieving younger students with average academically achieving older students. These teachers feel that the bright younger students are closer academically and socially with the older average students. An interesting contrast is that a few teachers (2%) feel that the top bright younger students should be grouped with the lower achieving older students.

It was found that 10% of the teachers felt that the students should be grouped heterogeneously. They said, "put the names in a hat and draw them out." These teachers contend that a wide range of abilities and social maturity is good. It makes the CC more nearly like a regular classroom.

A few teachers (8%) felt that the students should be grouped by their social maturity. This was found more often with the teachers who have older students. These teachers felt that the personal and social growth of students is important. These CC teachers sense that the socially mature students will cooperate and get along better than those who are less socially mature.

Miscellaneous suggestions (6%):

• Bright, self-disciplined, self-starting students in both grade levels
• Have no students in a CC that would go to some special teacher out of the room
• Have P.E., Music, Art, etc., scheduled so that it supported the CC instead of causing major problems
• Older students mixed in ability and lower students should be bright

- Both groups average in academic ability
- Teacher judgment or intuitions
- Principal's judgment or intuitions

The authors wondered whether using sociometric techniques to develop compatible groups for CCs would be a better way to group. The method was not mentioned by the CC teachers. It would seem that research should be done in this area to see if sociometric grouping could improve the effectiveness of a CC.

The results clearly tell us that there is no **one** universally agreed way to group students that the majority of the CC teachers agree upon. The item that received the strongest agreement was 27%. Table III shows how diverse the CC teachers' opinions were related to selecting students for a CC. It seems obvious that a long term longitudinal study needs to be conducted to determine the best ways to select students for a CC.

Table III
Selecting Students for Combination Classroom

Recommendations	Percentage Recommended
Have Responsibility	27%
High Academic Ability (both grades)	20%
Self-Disciplined	15%
High Achieving Younger Students and Average Achieving Older Students	14%
Heterogeneously	10%
Social Maturity	8%
Miscellaneous	6%

TEACHING TIPS FOR COMBINATION CLASSROOM TEACHING

The teachers in this survey gave us a wide range of tips on teaching in a CC. The number one suggestion was to integrate as much as is possible (22%). It was suggested that Language

Arts, Social Studies, Math and Science should be integrated more than is found in a regular classroom. By integrating one can combine grade levels and then teach as if it were a regular classroom. Integrating helps to eliminate the number of separate academic grade level classes that would need be taught. It is too time consuming to teach two separate academic grade level classes per day.

The use of Peer Tutors was recommended by 17% of the teachers. After the teacher has presented the material peer tutors can assist students on assignments. Review and practice activities can be handled by most good peer tutors. Tutors need to be taught how to assist other students properly.

Careful planning seems to be a needed skill for CC teachers (10%). Integrating was the most suggested teaching tip and in order to do it well one must plan carefully. Those teachers who are organized and plan well would seem better suited to teach a CC.

> **Integrating was the most suggested teaching tip and in order to do it well one must plan carefully.**

The use of centers was recommended by 8% of teachers. Centers allow for good classroom time management. Time seems to be the major problem of a CC teacher. The use of centers will free the teacher to teach small groups while other students are working alone or in small groups in centers. Peer tutors can assist students while they are in the centers. The use of centers requires careful planning as was suggested above.

Contracts were recommended as successful ways to let students work on their own (8%). Students are given a contract that is integrated and at their academic level. Assigning students varying lengths of time to complete the contract gives the teacher more flexibility. Keeping track of contracts takes careful planning. Peer tutors can assist students who are working on contracts.

Treat the CC as one grade level (8%). Do not teach two different grade level classes per day. Teach one lesson to the whole class. Do not separate the students by grade levels. This teaching tip goes along with integrating content, using peer tutors, careful planning, using centers and contracts. It is interesting to note that all of the teaching tips suggested to this point are compatible and support each other.

"Get a teaching assistant," was suggested by 6% of the teachers. They felt that with the added responsibility of a CC, a teaching assistant should given to all CC teachers.

Combine students together for all social activities (6%). This seems to develop the students socially better than when the students are kept apart by grade level. Having students together socially helps to develop class unity where the students work co-operatively together in the classroom. If peer tutoring is to be used, the classroom atmosphere needs to be one of cooperation. It seemed that the teachers who taught the upper grade students felt this way more often than the teachers from the lower grades.

It was suggested that the CC teacher not follow the text-books (5%). Instead they should use the standard course of study which is the state scope and sequence. Using the state scope allows for easier integration of academic content. If a teacher follows the teachers' edition of a textbook it can become very rigid and difficult to use when one wants to integrate. The state scope is easier to integrate at certain grade levels. This should be kept in mind by administrators when combining grade levels.

Be happy, flexible, relaxed and get enough sleep and rest was suggested by 4% of the teachers. When teachers are as-signed a CC for the first time they become nervous and up tight. "Relax and enjoy the children," was stated several times.

If you will have a CC again next year, keep the students from your lower grade level (3%). This will make it easier to condition your new students coming into your classroom. When half of the class knows what to do it takes less time to condition your new class. Having former students will save time in getting to know the new students and parents.

Do not assign teachers who are weak in discipline with CCs (3%). Good discipline is needed in a regular classroom but with a wider range of student maturity the class can become difficult to discipline. If cooperation between students is needed, then the way a teacher disciplines is important. Teachers who de-velop a democratic classroom and focus on self-discipline would be better for a CC.

To see more clearly the breakdown of teaching tips, look at Table IV. The table shows that the teachers who filled out the

Table IV
Teaching Tips for Combination Classroom Teachers

Recommendations	Percentages
Integrate Academic Areas	22%
Peer Tutors	17%
Careful Planning	10%
Centers	8%
Contracts	8%
Teach One Grade Level to Entire Class	8%
Integrate Socially	6%
Teaching Assistant	6%
Not to Follow Textbook	5%
Be Happy, Flexible, Relaxed	4%
Keep Younger Students Next Year	3%
Good Disciplinarian (self-discipline)	3%

questionnaire had a wide range of suggestions for CC teachers. The suggestions could be used by administrators to find teachers that have the skills and abilities to implement these suggestions in order to assign them to teach CCs.

A summary of these suggestions indicates that there is no one tip recommended by the majority of the CC teachers. It is interesting to note that all of the suggestions are compatible and can be used together in a CC. The results of this question are quite clear that a CC teacher must be an excellent organizer, planner and an expert in curriculum. The CC teachers suggested that all academic areas be integrated so that the students are taught as though they were all in the same grade. The teacher needs to integrate and not follow a basal textbook. The use of centers and contracts, peer tutors and teaching assistants can free the teacher to work with individuals or groups of students; this approach also requires good organizational skills. Teachers who develop self-disciplined students would develop better cooperation between the grade levels in a CC.

The teachers who are going to teach in CC would find a review of the literature on multi-aged grouping and continuous progress helpful. The process of integrating academic content and classroom management skills are explained in the multi-aged grouping materials.

If administrators would implement the following suggestions perhaps having a CC would be considered a reward instead of an undesirable assignment. The data from this questionnaire would suggest that administrators who have the task of assigning teachers to CC do the following:

a. select students for CCs by the students': (1) responsibility level (2) academic ability (3) self-discipline
b. look at the state scope and sequence to determine which grade levels are best to combine
c. assign teachers who are well organized and good at planning
d. do not assign teachers who are weak in classroom control
e. assign the more experienced teachers to CCs
f. assign the younger bright students with the average older students
g. give the CC teacher a teaching assistant

In summary it seems that there is no one best way to group students for a CC. If you are a beginning teacher you are more likely to be assigned a CC. Those who are assigned a CC should integrate the content and use many classroom management activities in order to free the teacher from large class instructional time. Hopefully those who have the responsibility to teach a CC and those who assign teachers to teach in CCs will find this study practical and useful.

The Nongraded Classroom in Practice

by Joan Gaustad

The basic elements of nongraded education—mixed-age grouping, continuous progress, integrated learning, and developmentally appropriate practice—can be put into practice in a multitude of ways. They can be adapted to suit the needs of large school systems with many primary classes and teachers, or those of isolated rural schools with a single teacher and a handful of children. They can be adjusted to fit individual teaching styles, the preferences of particular communities, and a wide variety of physical settings.

A DIFFERENT KIND OF STRUCTURE

A 1989 newspaper article on British Columbia's primary education reform illustrates a common misperception of nongraded education. It call the ungraded approach "a less structured form of learning" and quotes an elementary school principal as saying, "We have seen the product of unstructured programs and it is poor.... They want to throw my structure out and that will create chaos" (Tim Jones 1989).

Nothing could be further from the truth. At first glance, an uninformed observer might judge a graded classroom with children seated quietly in orderly rows of desks to be "more structured" than a nongraded classroom in which children move between learning stations, some chattering as they work together on projects, others reading in a corner or listening to music through headphones.

> The successful nongraded classroom isn't unstructured—it's just differently structured.

Excerpted from *Nongraded Education: Mixed-Age, Integrated, and Developmentally Appropriate Education for Primary Children*, p. 19–37, March 1992. Reprinted with permission.

But careful thought and planning underlie that apparent loose-ness. The successful nongraded classroom isn't unstructured—it's just differently structured.

THE FRAMEWORK FOR LEARNING: SCHOOL AND CLASS ORGANIZATION

Deciding how to group students and teachers is one of the first organizational steps in implementing nongraded education. Basic considerations are the number of people involved, the preferences of staff and parents, and the physical layout of the available classrooms.

Please note that the labels K, 1, 2, 3, and so forth are used merely for convenience; they would not exist in a nongraded program.

Determining Class Composition

Mixing ages. A nongraded class should, by definition, contain children varying in age by at least a year, but it may contain children of a larger age range. The Kentucky Department of Education (undated a) spells out the possible ways ages can be mixed. *Multi-year groups* may contain children from three or four different years of the primary program: the equivalent of the former K-2, 1-3, or K-3. *Dual-year* groups could contain children formerly designated K-1, 1-2, or 2-3. *Single-year* groups may contain children who are in the same year of the primary program, but range in age by two or three years.

Teachers and researchers disagree on the best way to mix ages. Teacher Randa Nachbar (1989) is among those who feel classes of five- and six-year-olds work wonderfully. However, some teachers feel strongly that five-year-olds should not be grouped with children any older, as they are developmentally still in the preoperational stage (Cushman 1990). John Campbell School in Selah, Washington, originally placed five-through eight-year-olds in the same class (T. Marjorie Oberlander 1989), but later dropped the five-year-olds from the combination to lighten the teacher's load (Willis 1991).

Montessori schools divide children into overlapping age groups: 1-3, 3-6, 6-9, and 9-12. The overlap acknowledges the developmental changes that occur around six and nine years of age, when some children move to the next cognitive stage earlier than others. Montessori teacher Mary Motz praises the social advantages for children of putting three years in one class, but agrees that it's more work than teaching just two years (Cushman).

Other Class-Assignment Criteria. Age is not the only criterion to consider in grouping children. Oberlander describes the criteria used at John Campbell School. To ensure that each room had a heterogeneous mix, children of perceived high, medium, and low ability were assigned to each class. "We also made sure that each teacher received some children in need of special education, some minority children, and a mix of girls and boys." Parents' preferences were also considered, which was relatively easy since John Campbell had graded as well as nongraded classrooms.

The Kentucky Department of Education (undated a) also mentions these factors, plus social considerations such as children's friendships, family relationships, and compatibility with the teacher.

Nachbar says of her K-1 classes, "My experience suggests that random selection works as well as any fixed criteria." The Jeffersontown Elementary School in Louisville, Kentucky, also assigns children randomly (KEA-AEL 1991).

The Lake George Elementary School in New York tried "separating students who needed more structure from more independent learners" (Cohen 1989b). This approach was dropped when staff realized it gave the segregated "problem pupils" less opportunity to interact with, and emulate, more mature peers.

Shirley Gidley, specialist for the Oregon 21st Century Schools Council, points out that the configuration chosen depends on the size of the school in addition to staff preferences. A small school's only option might be K-3, while a large urban school would have sufficient primary-age children to experiment with several possible combinations.

Family Grouping. A common option is to keep children in the same classroom grouping, with the same teacher, for more than one year. This is known as *family grouping* or, less often, as *teacher cycling*. For example, in New York's Central Park East Elementary School each class contains two "grade" levels, and children spend two years with the same teacher (Cushman). In

Arcadia Neighborhood Learning Center in Scottsdale, Arizona, which arranges students in K-2, 1-3, and 2-4 combinations, students stay in the same class for three years ("Arizona School Welcomes Change to Ungraded Primary" 1991).

This arrangement has advantages for both teachers and students. Only one-third of each teacher's students are new each year, which means only one-third as many new names, personalities and sets of abilities to learn. Students in their second or third year are "old hands" who can welcome the newcomers and help teach them the rules. Students are required to make fewer transitions, and discipline problems diminish due to the greater familiarity the teacher has with each child (Cushman).

> **Children with non-standard learning styles benefit from the diversity of teaching styles.**

Some students will take more or fewer than the "standard" number of years to finish the curriculum—for example, two or four years to complete the "1-3" span. This individual variation is less conspicuous when children remain in a class for more than one year and aren't expected to move on all at once.

Parents often have reservations about multiple-year classes, say Goodlad and Anderson:

> While parents agree that there are benefits in having their children with a strong teacher for more than a signal year, they abhor the thought of exposing their children to two or more years of contact with a weak teacher. The answer may lie in organizational devices such as team-teaching, which permits long-term relationships of children with teachers while also allowing a variety of adults to be involved.

Team Teaching

Team teaching, which is frequently associated with nongraded education, has many advantages. The larger pool of students yields more possibilities for creating subgroups for specific purposes. Children with nonstandard learning styles benefit from the diversity of teaching styles, and all the children can benefit from the particular strengths of different teachers—in art or science, for example.

Patterns and Frequency. The pattern and frequency of collaboration may vary with the school's physical layout and the preferences of the teachers. The five teachers in the nongraded program at John Campbell School decided to situate their classes in a large open area, which they felt was "advantageous for planning and visual contact" (Oberlander). At Public School 41 in Brooklyn, New York, teachers in "clusters" of three or four classrooms work together as "core teams." Clusters work together on special projects, and children may move back and forth between classrooms to join instruction groups (Cushman, Cohen 1989b).

London Elementary School, a small 100-student school just south of Cottage Grove, Oregon, places it K-2 and 3-5 students in two "homerooms" for half of each day. Homeroom students study all subjects together except reading and math. During the other half of the day, the teachers divide the students into small math and reading groups according to skill levels, without regard for age or year in school. Teachers report that the traditional "bossiness and bullying" of younger children by older ones has almost totally disappeared since the multiage classes were established (Janelle Hartman 1992).

Cooperative Planning. Whatever the physical setting, team teaching requires group planning time and constant communication among team members. Core team members at P.S. 41 share lunch and planning periods each day in order to share information about children and coordinate projects. Teachers at Arcadia Neighborhood Learning Center meet after school several times per week. Some teachers may find this group process difficult and uncomfortable. Shirley Gidley recommends training in group decision-making for teachers who are unfamiliar with the process.

Cushman quotes Central Park East Director Esther Rosenthal on the possibility of friction: "You have to be reasonable about the interpersonal stuff.... With collaborative work, you have to be constantly talking about what you're doing, and it gets to be a strain." Cushman says that other teachers who have teamed up agree that "the right match of chemistry and teaching styles can make all the difference in how it works."

An Option, Not a Necessity. Goodlad and Anderson support team and cooperative teaching approaches as "the most promising ways of organizing schools horizontally," but emphasize that teaming is not a "necessary concomitant" of nongrading. The Kentucky Department of Education (undated a) promotes team teaching as an option for those comfortable with it. A single teacher can successfully implement nongraded education in a self-contained classroom.

Collaboration can enable teachers to experiment with mixed-age grouping within a traditional structure. Teachers of single-age classes can coordinate with other teachers to create mixed-age groups for portions of days, or for occasional integrated projects. This can also serve as a transition stage to a completely nongraded structure.

Classroom Organization and Materials

The concepts of active, hands-on learning and flexible grouping determine the physical organization of the nongraded classroom. Rows of desks do not face one direction; instead, tables and chairs are scattered around the room, ready to be regrouped for activities with large or small groups of children. Permanent seat assignments are not made, but children typically have a cubby hole labeled prominently with their names for storing folders and personal materials. Supplies are shelved where children can reach them.

> The concepts of active, hands-on learning and flexible grouping determine the physical organization of the nongraded classroom.

"Learning Centers" are scattered around the room: tables holding math, science, and art materials; a sand table with plastic toys for pretend play; a cozy, carpeted library corner with bean-bag chairs and low shelves stacked with a variety of interesting books. Tables and chairs are arranged so that children may work on projects in groups or engage in solitary journal writing. The NAEYC recommends that activity centers be changed frequently to give children new things to do, and that children and teachers decide on new projects together (NAEYC).

A math learning center should contain a variety of manipulative materials, games, and puzzles. Cuisenaire rods, developed by Belgian teacher M. Georges Cuisenaire in the 1930s, are one of the best-known manipulative math materials. These are wooden rods one square centimeter across, ranging in length from one to ten centimeters, each length a different color. In experimenting with Cuisenaire rods, children can "discover" basic mathematical relationships (KEA-AEL).

Other examples of math materials include abacuses, balance scales with different weights, containers for measuring liquids, and colorful plastic geometric shapes that can be joined together, counted, and measured. Fortunately for school budgets, "You won't need twenty-five of everything, since most activities will only involve a few children at a time," notes Cushman. Materials as ordinary and inexpensive as bottle caps and popsicle sticks can serve as objects to sort and count.

Textbooks such as basal readers may be used, but they are not central. Many other attractive and interesting types of literature, at varied levels of difficulty, are available for children to choose, including multicultural and nonsexist materials. Maps, globes, computers, musical instruments, and listening equipment are desirable supplementary materials.

FLEXIBLE GROUPING STRATEGIES

Students in a nongraded classroom are grouped for instruction in many ways, some of which are also used in graded classrooms. The difference is in the *flexibility* of the grouping. Children are grouped for specific and temporary purposes, and frequently regrouped by different criteria.

Homogeneous Grouping

Even the greatest supporters of mixed-age and mixed-ability grouping agree some curricula are most effectively taught to children of similar experience and achievement. Goodlad and Anderson cite basic reading skills and arithmetic as principal examples. Homogeneous grouping for this purpose is *achievement grouping*. Math and reading groups in a nongraded school include children at the same developmental level regardless of age, possibly from different classrooms. Regrouping occurs frequently to accommodate students who advance in spurts.

Children who are homogeneous according to one criterion typically vary widely in other ways, so they may be assigned to other homogeneous groups determined by different factors. For example, *learning-style grouping* brings together students with a common learning style; *reinforcement grouping* brings together children who need extra practice on a specific skill or task; and *interest grouping* brings together those who share a common interest (Cushman).

Goodlad and Anderson mention a strategy developed by a Florida teacher; grouping according to independence in study skills. The group of children least advanced in terms of self-discipline needed considerable attention and assistance in planning work, while a middle group need a moderate amount of teacher supervision, and the most advanced group could work with minimum assistance.

Teachers developing the nongraded program at John Campbell School were particularly concerned about developmental differences for physical education classes. Their solution:

> Early in the year the teachers worked with the physical education specialist to analyze children's physical skills before regrouping them into different physical skills groups. For 30 minutes each days, one of these groups would go to P.E., two to music (different teachers), one to the library, and one to a class in personal safety and drug and alcohol awareness. The arrangement worked well. (Oberlander)

Primary teachers at Westmoreland School in Eugene, Oregon, plan to occasionally combine TAG (talented and gifted) children from all their classes in one homogeneous group. Gifted children "need the opportunity to work with other students who are talented and gifted," says teacher Carol Olson, "so they don't feel so isolated. Because frequently they're the only one in the room, or one of two."

Heterogeneous Grouping

Goodlad and Anderson make a distinction between subjects with an internal organization that must be mastered in sequence, such as math, and subjects whose content has no intrinsic order, such as science and social studies.

In science, for example, certain broad principles and processes must be understood, such as ecology; certain cognitive processes must be developed, such as interpreting facts; and specific study skills must be learned, such as how to use reference materials. In studying a topic together, students starting at different levels can learn these principles, develop these processes, and begin to master these skills or refine them to a greater degree. Learning to use the scientific method is a process that takes years, as comprehension gradually grows; the order in which topics are presented is not significant.

Cooperative Group Projects. Subjects like these lend themselves to heterogeneous group study in the form of cooperative projects. Tasks can be divided according to the skill level of the child. For example, if books are being made to display what the group has learned about a topic, younger children can create the illustrations while older children write the text and bind the book (Katz and others).

Working in this format yields a threefold benefit. Children learn about the topic, taking in as much as is comprehensible to them at their current level of understanding. They practice skills at their current level of ability—writing, drawing, organizing. Last but not least, they practice social skills and learn to work co-operatively. These teamwork skills will be valuable in adult life whether the child becomes a construction worker, an office assistant, or a medical researcher.

> Children learn about the topic, taking in as much as is comprehensible to them at their current level of understanding.

Katz and her associates point out several ways adults can encourage successful cooperation. For example, if a group of children is working on a play and the "producers" decide some younger classmates aren't good enough actors to participate, the teacher can suggest additional, simpler roles or point out special talents of the younger children.

Group Sharing and Individual Challenge. Music, art, and language contain specific skills that must be learned, but they also have a highly individual creative element. At the elementary level, "A single stimulus may be used for children of widely varying levels of development," say Goodlad and Anderson. For example, children of various ages and skill levels can draw pictures inspired by the same piece of music, each child equally challenged though they produce art work at widely different levels of sophistication.

Another example: the teacher can read a story or poem aloud, lead a group discussion on the experiences of the characters or the theme of the poem, then direct children to express their thoughts and feelings by writing or drawing in individual journals.

Problem-Solving Grouping. Grouping students to discuss an unsolved problem can be used in any subject area: literature, social studies, health (Cushman). For example, Westmoreland School teacher Terry Snyder leads a group of children aged five to eight in a two-stage group discussion, part of a unit on transportation with the specific goal of teaching categorization.

First comes a brainstorming session to name as many types of transportation as possible. Snyder asks each child in turn for ideas, writing them on the chalkboard with vigorous gestures that mimic the type of movement. Next, he challenges the group to think of different ways these types of transportation could be grouped together. Categories suggested by the children include muscle-powered transportation (pogo stick, swimming, and bicycle) and transportation through the air (jet plane, helicopter, hot air balloon).

Snyder comments later, "I tell you, during the lesson I forget who is who. And sometimes it'll be real surprising. One of the little fellows in the back row could go into third grade next year, and I forget he's a five-year-old. And one second grader is probably emotionally a four or five year old. You really can't tell, as a general rule."

During group discussions, teachers can foster cross-age interaction by directing questions and comments back and forth between children. Katz and her colleagues give some examples:

> The teacher might ask... 'What do you think about that, Annie?' Or, she can ask the group, 'Have you any suggestions for Jerome's project on lizards?' Such strategies indicate to the children that lines of communication can go from child to child as well as from child to teacher and teacher to child.

Heterogeneous Pairs. The extensive research on peer tutoring has shown the value of pairing children at different levels of development or achievement. This pairing can range from asking an older child to help a younger one write her name on a painting, to assigning a pair to a regular tutoring relationship.

Encouraging one child to read to another benefits both, as Nachbar (1989) describes. "The children learn so much from each other as well as from the books. Invariably, a first grader teaches a kindergartner some words. Their excitement with reading is contagious!"

Katz and her colleagues suggest that teachers encourage younger children to request help and advice from older students, and encourage older ones to assume responsibility for helping younger ones. However, they warn against exploiting older children as helpers to the extent that their own progress is impeded. They also recommend monitoring interactions to ensure that problems are not developing. "Occasionally, a teacher has to tone down excessive zeal on the part of a responsible older child who may take her responsibilities a little too seriously! It takes some children time to learn the distinction between being helpful and being domineering."

INTEGRATED CURRICULUM

Members of a primary school class write a letter to the school district, requesting that a school bus be parked in their school's parking lot for several days. During this time, they walk around the bus and climb aboard, inspect it thoroughly, and learn to identify its different parts. In the classroom they discuss traffic rules. Finally they construct their own "bus" out of cardboard. Every evening for weeks, the children's parents hear enthusiastic stories about the bus (Kantrowitz and Wingert).

These children have had an *integrated* learning experience. They used all their senses actively in learning about the bus—looking, listening, touching, smelling. They used verbal and written language skills, art skills, and group problem-solving skills in discussing it and building the model. The lesson connects with their lives outside the school, whether they ride a school bus themselves or simply see buses drive by on the street.

The term *integration* has different connotations in various education and research contexts. This Bulletin focuses on those aspects particularly relevant to primary education: that information is more easily learned and remembered when it is taught in a meaningful context, when it is relevant to the learner, when the learner takes an active role and uses multiple mind/body functions in learning. Shoemaker explores the spectrum of meanings in depth in the October 1989 OSSC Bulletin, *Integrative Education: A Curriculum for the Twenty-First Century.*

In discussing interdisciplinary instruction, Bondi notes that "the real" world is a world of issues, topics, problems, and situations—not disciplines, subjects or courses" (Shoemaker). It is hoped that integrated instruction will prepare students to apply their knowledge to real-world problems more effectively than does a differentiated curriculum.

Teaching Around Themes

Shoemaker distinguishes between two types of theme teaching: the *topic* approach and the *concept* approach. "Dinosaurs" is an example of a topic, while "extinction" is an example of a concept. "Using a topic as a theme provides a narrow area of study for a short period. Using a concept as a theme allows for a broad area of study in which many topics can be explored." Shoemaker strongly supports organizing curricula around conceptual themes.

> "'The real' world is a world of issues, topics, problems, and situations—not disciplines, subjects or courses."

For example, in the *Education 2000 Integrated Curriculum* developed by the Eugene School District, "communities" is one of six concepts chosen as major organizers for the curriculum. From the subordinate concept "cultures," primary teachers at Westmoreland Elementary School selected China and Mexico as topics to study and presented the unit to their combined classes as a trip around the world.

First, children made passports for themselves. Next, they went to one classroom designated as the "plane," where they were given souvenir wing pins (Obtained from a teacher whose daughter conveniently works for an airline company) and saw an "in-flight movie" about the countries they were going to visit. "As the children would rotate through the various rooms they would take trips to various countries," Olson explains. "And we would do lessons in art, science, and writing, from those various countries." As the children learned to count in several different languages, they gleefully challenged each other to do simple arithmetic using French, Korean, Japanese, and Chinese numbers.

Whole-Language Instruction
The whole-language approach, which developed out of "language experience" approaches of the sixties and seventies, shares many elements with thematic instruction. It asserts that literacy is best taught in the meaningful context of literature and communication, rather than as a series of isolated subskills to be mastered step by step. It regards all aspects of language development as interrelated and holds that children can learn to read and write naturally, just as they learned to listen and speak (Russell Gersten and Joseph Dimino 1990).

Real books—not basal readers or edited, simplified versions—are central to whole-language teaching. Teachers should frequently read aloud to children, presenting them with exciting and engaging stories, playful rhymes to recite together, and colorful illustrations to look at. The teaching of subskills such as phonics can be integrated into this enjoyable sharing.

According to Gersten and Dimino, research indicates that the whole-language approach alone is insufficient for some students. While communicating the joy of reading is important, many students also need systematic, step-by-step instruction on the component skills, repeated practice, and specific feedback.

The NAEYC endorses an integrated approach to the teaching of language and literacy that includes many elements of the whole-language approach. The association supports teaching subskills as needed to individual children and small groups, accepting children's invented spellings, and teaching literacy skills in the context of projects in other content areas.

ASSESSMENT AND EVALUATION
Primary teacher Terry Snyder recalls seeing an endless series of committees struggle to revise report card formats during his twenty years in education. In his opinion, the limited alternatives on report card checklists "never match what's really going on, especially with small children. You look at so many different components, and it's not a black-and-white thing."

The NAEYC agrees with Snyder, discouraging the use of letter or numerical grades for primary children as "inadequate reflections of children's ongoing learning" (NAEYC). This section examines some alternative, qualitative methods of assessment commonly used in nongraded primary programs. The Kentucky Department of Education (undated a) describes such methods as "authentic assessment—an assessment of what we actually want students to be able to do or understand."

It should be remembered that assessment by qualitative methods is not necessarily linked with nongraded class organization. Some nongraded classes use grades for assessment, while some graded classes use qualitative methods.

Narrative Descriptions of Student Progress

A variety of organizations and educators recommend assessing student progress by observation and regular recording of narrative comments, also called anecdotal records or reports. Records can also be made using other methods, such as audiotape or videotape.

> Collecting samples of children's work over time provides vivid and concrete evidence of progress.

Goodlad and Anderson urge teachers to record specific, *descriptive* comments as opposed to general or judgmental statements. For example, the comments "Jimmy is now reading with fewer pauses for word recognition than several months back" and "he is learning to write the more difficult letters (such as n, r, d, e) in less time" are more accurate and useful than "Jimmy is doing well in reading" and "his handwriting is getting better" (Goodlad and Anderson).

Collections of Students' Work

Collecting samples of children's work over time provides vivid and concrete evidence of progress. In addition to samples of the child's best work—some selected by the teacher, some by the child—Westmoreland School portfolios also contain children's personal background information, standardized test scores, notes on their level of achievement in various curriculum areas and on any special enrichment or remediation programs in which they are participating.

Westmoreland teacher Carol Olson displays a simple but ingenious assessment tool kept in the portfolio: a sheet of white paper containing four columns of ten lines each, folded over and taped shut so that only one column is visible. A spelling test of the same ten dictated words is given four times per year, each time with the sheet folded to reveal a different blank column. Unfolding the sheet dramatically reveals a child's progress over the course of the year—from a few straggling letters written almost at random, to mastery of most letters with guessed or invented spellings, to neater printing and a greater number of standard spellings.

Conferences with Parents and Children

Parent conferences are a form of progress reporting particularly important for nongraded programs. Finding time and space for face-to-face conferences can be a challenge, however. Scheduling conferences after school or in the evening cuts into the teacher's personal time, dismissing school cuts into lesson time, and providing substitutes to free teachers for conferences is expensive.

Goodlad and Anderson note that dismissing school early a specified number of afternoons per year is more popular with parents than dismissing school for an entire day or afternoon, and also avoids "running afoul of the attendance laws in many states, where a 'day' must be a certain length." They also suggest providing teachers with inservice training in both oral and written reporting techniques.

Frequent informal conferences with children are an important part of nongraded education. These need not be formally scheduled conferences, just a few quiet minutes of conversation in a corner. Talking with children helps teachers discover how they feel about their own progress and about any problems they may be having. Primary age children may be excessively self-critical; they need realistic feedback and encouragement on tasks they are finding difficult, as well as praise and acknowledgment for their achievements. Conversations with the teacher help them learn to evaluate themselves constructively and to set appropriate individual goals (Ministry of Education 1991c).

Comparing Individual Progress to General Norms

A continuous progress format without competitive pressure may optimize children's learning, but parents will still want to know how their children are progressing compared to others. To give both teachers and parents a frame of reference, the Ministry of Education (1991c) of the province of British Columbia has developed listings of "widely held expectations" for children's development in physical, social, emotional, intellectual, and artistic areas, as well as in the specific curriculum areas of mathematics and reading.

Charts describe behavior, skills, and concepts children usually master within certain age ranges, rather than listing specific achievements expected of all children by specific ages. Parents can see how their child's progress compares to these general normative ranges, while being encouraged to accept that some variation from area to area is normal. This also avoids better-or-worse comparisons with the child's classmates.

Accountability and Testing

Public concern about the shortcomings of the educational system has resulted in increased demands for accountability on the part of schools, districts, and individual teachers. Evidence of improvement in student performance is being called for at local, state, and national levels. Teachers, school boards, and parents want quantitative measures that will enable them to evaluate the comparative effectiveness of different instructional approaches.

In the past, improvement in student performance has usually been equated with higher standardized test scores. Standardized tests may provide a useful standard of comparison, at least once children have reached the age at which test results are valid. As was previously described, test scores of students in nongraded programs generally equal those of students in graded programs.

> Many educators and other citizens are troubled about the limited information and skills that standardized tests are capable of measuring.

However, many educators and other citizens are troubled about the limited information and skills that standardized tests are capable of measuring. A child who can correctly indicate which one of four words is misspelled can't necessarily write a coherent paragraph (Kantrowitz and Wingert); a student who can perform rote mathematical calculations may be unable to apply those skills in real-world problem-solving (Fran Salyers 1991). Educators are searching for new types of testing that measure the ability to apply skills and knowledge.

The Kentucky Department of Education is developing a new, primarily performance-based, assessment system called the Kentucky Instructional Results Information System, or KIRIS.

KIRIS consists of three main types of assessment. First is the evaluation of student portfolios, as described above. Second, KIRIS will give students "assessment tasks" that require them "to use knowledge and skills learned in school to produce a product or solve a problem. Rather than recall facts, students will apply what they have learned to a real situation" (Thomas C. Boysen 1991). The third component of KIRIS is a paper-and-pencil examination modeled after those created by the National Assessment of Educational Progress. This test will use some multiple choice and some open-ended questions to assess students' ability to use "higher-order thinking skills...reasoning, analytical and written communication skills" (Boysen).

Kentucky is only mandating this "accountability assessment" after the primary level, starting in grade 4, but it encourages voluntary assessment of a similar type at the primary level. Nongraded instruction that uses active, integrated learning should increase students' ability to apply their knowledge in the manner KIRIS will assess.

Qualitative and performance-based types of assessment may be more time-consuming to administer and evaluate. Computer-graded multiple-choice exams are much easier and more efficient to administer and analyze. But as Goodlad and Anderson point out, "Efficiency takes on proper meaning only in relation to the job that should be done. To recognize that something is easy does not justify our doing it."

CONCLUSION: A QUESTION OF BALANCE

Kantrowitz and Wingert quote Illinois professor Lilian Katz as saying "People think that school has to be either free play or all worksheets. The truth is that neither is enough. There has to be a balance between spontaneous play and teacher-directed work."

This theme of balance runs through all the elements that make up the nongraded classroom. A balanced mixture of ages and abilities is important in determining class composition.

Then the teacher must guide interactions to ensure that younger children don't become too dependent, nor the older children too bossy. Collaborating teachers must balance their personal needs and preferences against those of the team as a whole.

In structuring the school day, teachers must vary sizes and types of grouping—large and small, homogeneous and heterogeneous, high-energy and quiet time. The shared pleasure of reading aloud must be leavened with individual instruction and feedback. Staff at P.S. 41 and Lake George Elementary School strive to balance structured activities with those that offer children choices (Cohen 1989b).

Miller (1989) feels establishing "a context of clear rules and routines" is vital to the success of the multiage classroom. Within this secure and predictable structure, children can enjoy having the freedom to explore individual interests. And with their individual differences accepted, they can find a true sense of community in their classroom, not just an enforced conformity.

Teaching and Learning in the Multigrade Classroom
Student Performance and Instructional Routines

by Bruce Miller

The multigrade classroom is an organizational pattern widely used in schools in the United States. Typically a feature of small-scale schooling, multigrade classrooms are today getting a closer look. This Digest, written for practitioners, parents, and policymakers, brings together recent information on the topic. It considers the history of the multigrade classroom, its effects on achievement and attitude, and the requirements of teaching and learning in multigrade classrooms.

HISTORY AND BACKGROUND

In 1918, there were 196,037 one-room schools, representing 70.8 percent of all public schools in the United States. By 1980, less than 1,000 of these schools remained (Muse, Smith, & Barker, 1987). But the multigrade classroom persists. For example, in a study consisting of multigrade classrooms of only two grades, Rule (1983) used a sample from a suburban district outside Phoenix, Arizona. Of the 21,000 elementary students in the district, approximately 17 percent were in classrooms that combined grades. In rural, small elementary schools the incidence of students served in multigrade classrooms may well be much higher.

Although rural, small schools may combine grades to save money, in the guise of the "ungraded classroom," multigrade organization has also been a feature of urban and suburban districts. In the 1960s and 1970s, "open education" and individualized instruction became influential curriculum and instruc-

From *ERIC Clearinghouse on Rural Education and Small Schools*, Charleston, WV. (EDO-RC-91-6), May 1991. Reprinted with permission.

tional models. Such models were commonly implemented with multigrade classrooms. Energized by development theories of learning, a large influx in federal money, and student-centered models of instruction, open education became a major educational innovation. As a result, multigrade classrooms received new attention.

Numerous studies compared the effectiveness of "open" classrooms (multigrade organization with student-centered ethos and methods) and "regular" classrooms (single-grade organization with traditional ethos and methods). We have a learned a great deal from these innovative efforts. Working in an open, multigrade school requires serious, ongoing teacher training and a commitment to hard work.

> **Working in an open, multigrade school requires serious, ongoing teacher training and a commitment to hard work.**

Most teachers have been trained to work in single-grade classrooms. Their knowledge of teaching method is based on whole-class instruction and small-group instruction (with groups often formed on the basis of ability or achievement level). When placed in a multigrade setting, teachers of the 60s and 70s discovered that the time requirements and skills needed to be effective were simply *not part of their prior training and experience.* Although the premises of "open" and "regular" (traditional) education can differ sharply, this finding still applies to multigrade classrooms in traditional schools.

THE NORM OF THE GRADED SCHOOL

The large-scale innovations of the 60s and 70s have virtually ended. But the multigrade classroom persists, especially in small, rural schools. Yet, here as elsewhere, most people view graded schools as the *natural way to organize education.* This norm can be a handicap for anyone (whether out of necessity or by theoretical design) who wants to—or who must—work with multigrade classrooms or schools. Teachers of multigraded classrooms who face the biggest challenge may be those working in school systems in which single-grade classrooms are the norm.

For many rural educators, multigrade instruction is not an experiment or a new educational trend, but a necessity imposed, in part, by economic and geographic conditions. In an environment dominated by graded schools, the decision to combine grades can be quire difficult—especially if constituents feel shortchanged by the decision. Nonetheless, recent proposals for school restructuring reflect renewed interest in multigrade organization (Cohen, 1989) and in small-scale organization generally. Such work may eventually contest the norm of the graded school.

EFFECTS ON STUDENT PERFORMANCE

Many teachers, administrators, and parents continue to wonder whether or not multigrade organization has negative effects on student performance. Research evidence indicates that being a student in a multigrade classroom does not negatively affect academic performance, social relationships, or attitudes.

Miller (1990) reviewed 13 experimental studies assessing academic achievement in single-grade and multigrade classrooms and found there to be no significant differences between them. The data clearly support the multigrade classroom as a viable and *equally effective* organizational alternative to single-grade instruction. The limited evidence suggests there may be significant differences depending on subject or grade level. Primarily, these studies reflect the complex and variable nature of school life. Moreover, there are not enough such studies to make safe generalizations about which subjects or grade levels are best for multigrade instruction.

When it comes to student affect, however, the case for multigrade organization appears much stronger. Of the 21 separate measures used to assess student affect in the studies reviewed, 81 percent favored the multigrade classroom (Miller, 1990).

If this is the case, why then do we have more schools organized into multigrade classrooms? One response is that history and convention dictate the prevalence of graded classrooms. However, there is a related, but more compelling, answer to be found in the classrooms themselves and in information drawn from classroom practitioners.

INSTRUCTIONAL AND ORGANIZATIONAL ROUTINES

The multigrade classroom can be more of a challenge than the single-grade classroom. Skills and behavior required of the teacher may be different, and coordinating activities can be more difficult. In fact, such a realization is one reason graded schools came into being in the first place (Callahan, 1962).

At first look, the skills needed to teach well in the multi-grade and the single-grade (multilevel) classroom appear to be quite similar. The differences between the two sorts of classrooms may be more a product of socialization and expectation than of fact. Clearly, if a teacher in either sort of classroom fails to address differences among students, the effectiveness of instruction suffers. Likewise, teachers are harmed when they have not been adequately prepared to teach students with varying ages and abilities—no matter what sort of classroom they work in.

> If a teacher in either sort of classroom fails to address differences among students, the effectiveness of instruction suffers.

But what does the research tell us regarding the skills required of the multigrade teacher? When student diversity increases, whether it be in a multigrade or single-grade classroom, greater demand is placed on teacher resources, both cognitive and emotional.

Six key instructional dimensions affecting successful multi-grade teaching have been identified from multigrade classroom research (Miller, 1991). Note that each of these points has some bearing on the related issues of independence and interdependence. It is important to cultivate among students the habits of responsibility for their own learning, but also their willingness to help one another learn.

1. **Classroom organization:** Instructional resources and the physical environment to facilitate learning.

2. **Classroom management and discipline:** Classroom schedules and routines that promote clear, predictable instructional patterns, especially those that enhance student responsibility for their own learning.

3. **Instructional organization and curriculum:** Instructional strategies and routines for a maximum of cooperative and self-directed student learning based on diagnosed student needs. Also includes the effective use of time.

4. **Instructional delivery and grouping:** Methods that improve the quality of instruction, including strategies for organizing group learning activities across and within grade levels.

5. **Self-directed learning:** Students' skills and strategies for a high level of independence and efficiency in learning individually or in combination with other students.

6. **Peer tutoring:** Classroom routines and students' skills in serving as "teachers" to other students within and across differing grade levels.

In the multigrade classrooms, more time must be spent in organizing and planning for instruction. Extra materials and strategies must be developed so that students will be meaningfully engaged. This additional coordination lets the teacher meet with small groups or individuals, while other work continues.

Since the teacher cannot be everywhere or with each student simultaneously, the teacher shares instruction responsibilities with students. *A context of clear rules and routines* makes such shared responsibility productive. Students know what the teacher expects. They know what assignments to work on, when they are due, how to get them graded, how to get extra help, and where to turn assignments in.

Students learn how to help one another and themselves. At an early age, students are expected to develop independence. The effective multigrade teacher establishes a climate to promote and develop this independence. For example, when young students enter the classroom for the first time, they receive help and guidance not only from the teacher, but from older students. In this way, they also learn that *the teacher is not the only source of knowledge.*

Instructional grouping practices also play an important role in a good multigrade classroom. The teacher emphasizes the similarities among the different grades and teaches to them, thus conserving valuable teacher time. For example, whole-class (cross-grade) instruction is often used since the teacher can have contact with more students. However, whole-class instruction in the effective multigrade classroom differs from what one generally finds in a single-grade class.

Multigrade teachers recognize that whole-class instruction must revolve around open task activities if all students are to be engaged. For example, a teacher can introduce a writing assignment through topic development where all students "brainstorm" ideas. In this context, students from all grades can discuss different perspectives. They can learn to consider and respect the opinions of others (Miller, 1989).

Cooperation is a necessary condition of life in the multigrade classroom. All ages become classmates, and this closeness extends beyond the walls of the school to include the community.

Rewards and Challenges

There are many rewards for teaching in the multigrade classroom, but there are challenges, too. Instruction, classroom organization, and management are complex and demanding. A teacher cannot ignore development differences in students nor be ill-prepared for a day's instruction. Demands on teacher time require well-developed organizational skills.

The multigrade classroom is not for the timid, inexperienced, or untrained teacher. Clearly, the implications for teacher educators, rural school board members, administrators, and parents are far-reaching.

REFERENCES

Callahan, R. (1962). *Education and the cult of efficiency.* Chicago: University of Chicago Press.

Cohen, D. (1989). First stirrings of a new trend: Multigrade classrooms gain favor. *Education Weeks, 9*(14), 1, 13-15.

Miller, B. (1991). A review of the qualitative research on multigrade instruction. *Research in Rural Education, 7*(2), 3-12.

Miller, B. (1990). A review of the quantitative research on multigrade instruction. *Research in Rural Education, 7*(1), 1-8.

Miller, B. (1989). *The multigrade classroom: A resource handbook for small, rural schools.* Portland, OR: Northwest Regional Educational Laboratory (ERIC Document Reproduction Service No. ED 320 719).

Muse, I., Smith, R., & Barker, B. (1987). *The one-teacher school in the 1980s.* Las Cruces, NM: ERIC Clearinghouse on Rural Education and Small Schools. (ERIC Document Reproduction Service No. ED 287 646).

Rule, J. (1983). Effects of multigrade grouping on elementary student achievement in reading and mathematics. *Dissertation Abstracts International, 44*(3), 662. (University Microfilms No. ADG 83-15672).

Prepared by Bruce Miller, Northwest Regional Educational Laboratory, Portland, OR.

High Expectations for Multi-Age Classrooms

by Robert H. Anderson, Robin Fogarty, Gina Rae, Carolyn Chapman, and Linda Schrenko

N ongradedness: Helping the Right Things to Happen to Kids

by Robert Anderson

A welcome by-product of the current dialogue about the need for fundamental changes in schooling is an invigorated interest in modifying the familiar but outdated pattern of self-contained teachers following a strictly defined, graded curriculum with children of the same age. Nongradedness, an alternative that has been around in various forms for over one hundred years, has come back into focus as a necessary arrangement if schools are to meet the wide range and increasing complexity of pupil needs. The articles by Jeannie Oakes and Robert Slavin, in the Fall 1992 issue of HIGH EXPECTATIONS, are representative of recent writings and research reports to the effect that changes of the sort more readily nurtured in a nongraded environment are long overdue.

Labels that are now in common use, such as nongradedness, team teaching, multi-age grouping, cooperative learning, and interdisciplinary curriculum, have different meanings for practitioners, researchers, and lay citizens. Furthermore, there are dozens of legitimate though different interpretations and combinations of the ideas behind these terms. This is probably healthy, although in conversations and in research projects it is very important to make clear the definition(s) to which one is committed.

From *High Expectations*, vol. 1, no. 2, p. 1–8, Winter 1993. Reprinted with permission.

In my own view, nongradedness is the antonym of gradedness: no lock-step progression through rigidly defined levels (1st Grade, 2nd Grade, etc.), no ABCDEF competitive-comparative assessment system, no norm-referenced promotion and retention system. In further defining what I do *not* value, the literal self-containment of teachers and the limitation of class groupings to pupils of roughly the same chronological age.

AN IDEAL

In other words, an "ideal" organizational pattern would find a heterogeneous collection of children representing at least two (preferably three) age cohorts living and learning together, in the charge of three to five teachers who function as a team. Each child progresses according to his or her optimum timetable and learning capacities, and all children experience a rich, well-integrated curriculum in a variety of sequences that permit extensive sharing and collaboration. All of this, and more, happening within a district-wide framework that encourages and supports diversity and experimentation.

It seems that the atmosphere in the country is now more favorable to making fundamental changes in schooling than perhaps it has ever been.

It seems that the atmosphere in the country is now more favorable to making fundamental changes in schooling than perhaps it has ever been, as witness the national attention to school reform and the enactment in numerous states of legislation calling for replacement of the old structures. Researchers are accelerating their efforts, and the literature is expanding rapidly.

In addition, there is so much interest in exploring nongradedness that we have created an International Registry of Nongraded Schools (IRONS) so that such explorations can be guided by specific information about what other schools are doing. In this latter effort, it will be necessary to identify (a) schools that have reasonably "authentic" nongraded programs already in place and (b) schools that have made a commitment but are just getting started. (For more information on IRONS, write Robert H. Anderson, P.O. Box 271669, Tampa, FL 33688-1669.)

STATE-OF-THE-ART LEARNING

Nongradedness is not an end in itself, since how a school is organized is far less important than what happens both psycho-emotionally and intellectually to children within the school environment. I will welcome the day when the graded structure has been totally abandoned, when teachers no longer work in isolation from each other, when pupil assessment will be authentic and noncompetitive, and when children have maximum opportunity to interact with each other across the full spectrum of human uniqueness. Then, at last, seeking and exploiting opportunities for implementing a topflight curriculum within a state-of-the-art learning environment might become our primary focus.

The One-Room Schoolhouse

by Robin Fogarty

Imagine a multi-age grouping of fifty-four, eight to twelve year olds, with two teachers in a double room with a folding wall and you have a picture of an innovative teaching experience. Enter the world of KINC., our abbreviated logo for Kids Incorporated.

Grounded in the development psychology of Piaget and the educational philosophy of Dewey, a first grade teacher and a fifth grade teacher draft a proposal for the board of education to create an alternative school within a school. What follows is a classroom in which the learners are the focus of every interaction. To illustrate the inner workings of this schoolroom "family," I write a few selected anecdotes about our world of kids.

Quite early, in the fall of the year, an outdoor education week at Stronghold Castle is the focus of much energy. This excursion involves all the children, as well as many of their parents. Students pre-register for classes of their choice. Their selections include: *The Cemetery Study*, a Renaissance approach to a Civil War cemetery visit in which history, literature, art, and psychology are integrated; or *Robinson Crusoe*, an overnight camping trip in which they make and sleep under a lean-to; or

Tippecanoe and Tyler, Too, a canoeing class held in the resident swimming pool; or *Use Your Noodles*, a nutrition class in which students learn about good foods to fuel the body and then make blue, green, and red noodles for the lunch meal of soup and sandwiches. The overriding purpose of this affair is to build the diverse group of eight to twelve year olds into a coherent and caring team.

The kids in KINC. are grouped and regrouped for basic subjects by skill level. Students take a series of pretests in math and reading and, regardless of age, are placed in appropriate skill-building groups for targeted instruction. In addition, there is a silent reading time in which kids read from basal readers, anthologies, or library books of their choice. Science and social studies are approached through themes such as WATER or ELECTRICITY; WAR or WESTWARD MOVEMENT. Students select topics of interest within the umbrella themes and work in multi-age groups to do prearranged experiments or projects.

> The overriding purpose of this affair is to build the diverse group of eight to twelve year olds into a coherent and caring team.

A final glimpse into this one-room schoolhouse focuses on the collegial partnership that develops into a caring, effective, balanced, and creative teaching team. In KINC., the opportunity for ongoing professional dialogue is a natural focus. In fact, the conversations are not only necessary for the routine planning stages, but they are coveted for the therapeutic processing they afford. It is in these daily, verbal meanderings that illumination and insight occur. It is through the mirroring of each other's thoughts that reflective practice develops.

The concept of a family grouping, the one-room schoolhouse, where ages cluster, stray, and straggle across traditional grades and age groups is a natural setting in which to frame learning. And, the added benefits of providing teachers with the chance to work in partnerships enhance the model of lifelong learning for children and adults alike.

trategies That Work in Nongraded Classrooms

by Gina Rae

In Richmond, British Columbia, teachers are in the process of incorporating strategies and developing structures that work in nongraded classrooms. Most teachers agree that with adequate support in place, every child can be part of a classroom community where opportunities are provided to learn in a variety of ways at a level and rate that is personally challenging. The following examples from two Richmond classrooms illustrate the kinds of strategies and structures that can be used with diverse learners to promote continuous progress.

Classrooms like the ones described [here] allow for easy access to interesting learning experiences and challenge students to take their assignment as far as they can. Grouping arrangements are flexible and varied. Children who benefit from some small group or individual work with an adult in a quiet place get what they need, but they work on personalized classroom assignments—not special remedial tasks.

Teachers like these are comfortable with direct instruction and teaching skills, but skills are taught in context. For example, spelling and proofreading skills are taught as a natural outgrowth of the writing process.

Classrooms like these allow for choice. Children have a say in which topics they will write about on research, which books they will read, and which class they will work with on certain projects.

These nongraded classrooms reflect far more than simply a way of grouping students for learning. They reflect a philosophical stance toward children as learners that is based on a professional respect for the uniqueness of each individual, while acknowledging and building on the characteristics that all learners share in common.

WRITER'S WORKSHOP
Adam Heeny and Julie White team teach in a large double classroom at Bridge Elementary School. Their group includes fifty 7,
8, 9, and 10 year olds. Based on beliefs about teaching children
and writing shared by Graves, Calkins, Atwell, and others,
Adam and Julie have created their own unique version of the
Writer's Workshop. They use a very simple, predictable structure that includes the following elements:

Status-of-the-Class Wall Chart
Encourage independence...
Each day students fill in which stage of writing process they are
presently working on beside their name. Then they get their
writing folders and begin working.

Provide for choice...
On a given day, an individual may be starting a new piece, planning, prewriting, drafting, self- or peer editing, conferencing
with the teacher, proofreading, publishing, or illustrating.

Writing Folders
Provide organization...
Past drafts, current work, and published pieces are organized
and accessible to each student. The natural portfolios are ongoing artifact collections.

Mini Lessons
Teach skills and strategies directly...
Brief daily lessons dealing with selected aspects of the writing
process that will be helpful to students are taught. Lessons focus
on topics such as getting started, writing leads, editing, proofreading, note taking, spelling, and publishing.

Editing
Encouage students to learn from each other...
Students reread their own drafts, share drafts with a partner,
and conference with the teacher.

Conferences
Appreciate the writing...
Teachers conference on the fly and schedule longer talks with
certain students each day. For some children, more frequent
conferences are needed.

Sharing
Value each writer...
Two or three pieces in progress are heard by the whole class each day. Comments and questions discussed in the large group set the tone for future peer conferencing in pairs.

Predictable Structure
Provide structure...
A calm but busy workshop atmosphere results from this well-organized structure with its clear ground rules. Children are free to write on self-selected topics in a variety of genres. Each child is engaged in the writing process at his or her own pace and stage of development.

Adequate Support
Work with individuals and small groups...
In addition to the daily involvement of the classroom teachers, the Resource Teacher and Classroom Assistant are on hand to work with individuals or small groups as needed. Direct instruction and careful monitoring contribute over time to a productive workshop atmosphere as well as the quality of writing produced.

Stretch the learning...
Ongoing participation in the Writer's Workshop builds writing know-how and skill that can be applied to written work across the curriculum as well as independent research projects.

INTEGRATED STUDIES
Elsie Chan, at DeBeck Elementary School, enjoys designing integrated learning experiences. She believes that working with rich content and providing open-ended assignments stimulates high quality of work from all her students. Her approach to teaching an integrated unit on geography emphasizes the following elements:

Rich Content/Complex Concepts
Teach the whole class...
Elsie's class of 7, 8, and 9 year olds are learning how to identify a long list of geographic features such as island, volcano, delta, valley, creek, river, and so on.

Design open-ended assignments…
For their first assignment, students are asked to create an imaginary island incorporating as many of the geographic features under study as they can.

Integration
Represent learning through the arts…
As each student works out his or her own imaginative illustration, opportunities to learn about scale and direction present themselves.

Look for natural links with other subjects…
These concepts are directly taught and applied to the imaginary maps. For their next assignment, students are asked to make up questions about their maps and quiz each other in pairs.

Use cooperative learning…
Questions like these are asked and answered: How many kilometers is it from Chocolate Creek to Round Lake? If you climb down the volcano road and look south, southwest, what two cities do you see that are 10 kilometers away?

Creating Responsible Learners
Provide opportunities for transfer…
The knowledge of geographic features acquired is then applied to a homework assignment. Students are asked to create a salt and flour dough map of their imaginary island on cardboard and paint it.

Encourage self-monitoring and self-evaluation…
A step-by-step checklist and self-evaluation form is provided to guide the children through this multistep project and encourage them to monitor their own efforts. At various stages, the project is discussed in class.

Sharing
Celebrate accomplishments…
On the due date, the three-dimensional maps are brought to school and displayed on each desk along with the hand-drawn maps and other written assignments.

Value artistry and quality…
The maps are mounted on brown paper with singed edges to resemble ancient artifacts.

Verbalize the learning…
The assignment that day is for students to give guided tours of their islands to visitors from another class and to answer their questions. The visitors' assignment is to ask interesting questions.

As a result of these carefully orchestrated experiences, Elsie's students are able to apply their developing skills and their knowledge and understanding of geographic features to future studies and research projects.

Multiple Intelligences: If the Shoe Fits…

by Carolyn Chapman and Linda Schrenko

Today's classroom requires that the teacher adapt his or her teaching methods to meet the diverse challenges of today's students. Nongraded classrooms provide the perfect setting in which to do this. When we begin to think of students as diversely intelligent rather than measuring every child against one fixed standard (IQ), we measure everyone realistically.

For teachers, this means assessing our students, determining their intelligences, and planning activities to enhance those intelligences. But is that enough? Is it not also our mission as teachers to allow students to awaken dormant or weaker intelligences and help students to grow and learn in different ways?

By setting up a curriculum that taps into multiple intelligences rather than one or two, we give all students a fair chance to reach their potential. Giving students freedom to move into their discomfort zones, expand their options, and enjoy the process, provides a more realistic way of teaching and learning. Every child can learn. It is up to us as educators to engage their full intellectual potential.

THE LEARNER   THE LEARNING METHOD

Bodily/Kinesthetic—Athletic Shoe

Joan has a highly developed bodily kinesthetic intelligence. When a ball is thrown to her, she reacts well, judging distance and maneuvering to be at the right place at the right time. Joan needs an athletic shoe.

In class she needs a physical environment with hands-on experience using manipulatives, classroom games, creative movement, role play, frequent exercise breaks, and field trips. Joan may need to stroll the halls with her book or rock in the rocking chair during reading time.

Visual/Spatial—Cinderella's Slipper

Kay, our doodler, is visual spatial. She is creative, seeing the world in terms of pictures and colors. Her doodling may actually be the channel through which she internalizes what is being said. Her shoe looks like Cinderella's slipper because of her creative imagination. She invents in order to learn.

Kay responds well to graphs, colors, and pictures. She is able to understand and interpret more easily when she draws a picture than when she reads a book. Highlighting in color may help her. She needs time to imagine, create, and visualize.

Interpersonal—Football Team Cleats

Dave has a highly developed interpersonal intelligence, loving his fellow students and appreciating their diversities (differences). He likes to study people in other cultures as well as their art and history.

In the classroom Dave excels in cooperative learning groups. He works well with partners and tries hard to help those in his group. He does well with team projects, peer tutoring, and other forms of learning that use his social strengths.

Musical/Rhythmic—Drum Major's Boot

Bonnie's highly developed intelligence is musical. She is tuned in to the sounds and rhythms around her, and responds by action sometimes. Hers is a world of melody and beat.

Bonnie's classroom must include the use of music to introduce selections and stories. Allow her time to create songs. Use different pitch and tone to create emotional attitudes, and include background music to keep her "tuned in."

Intrapersonal—Warm, Fuzzy Bedroom Slipper

Our intrapersonally intelligent child is Rose, who seldom participates in class discussions or social activities. She seems to live in her own world of daydreams and yet astounds us with her insight and interpretation.

Her ability to understand herself and others, to set and achieve her goals, and to learn independently are strengths in the classroom. Rose responds to creating her own poems or legends to explain the mysteries of life. Her journal may be the key to tapping into her thoughts and feelings.

Logical/Mathematical—Hiking Boot

Roy has a highly developed logical mathematical intelligence. He is good at calculations, problem solving, critical thinking, interpreting, categorizing facts and information, and using technology.

Roy does well with opportunities to explore in lab situations, solve problems, research, organize, and present information and reports. Technology will keep him interested and motivated.

Verbal/Linguistic—Tap Shoe

Jeff, our verbal linguistically intelligent student, thinks well in words and expresses himself beautifully. He fits well in the traditional classroom because of his strengths in reading, writing, and speaking.

To assist Jeff in the classroom is easy. Any writing assignment, discussion, debate, or reading assignment interests Jeff. Our challenge is to develop other intelligences to help him become a well-rounded person.

Parents: An Essential Part of the Learning Team

by Linda Schrenko

A look at the research shows that parental involvement in any school is a critical element of success, but as we look toward nongraded schools, the parent factor becomes even more essential.

As teachers search for the most appropriate approaches to ensure student learning, the conventional graded structure of the traditional school simply does not fit the individual differences of the child and inhibits the teacher's ability to deal with them. A more logical approach is a multi-age classroom that allows flexible grouping and team teaching. The possibilities for reaching children are endless, but a word of caution is needed. In order for any system to work, parents must first understand and then support it.

I suggest that a teacher investigating the nongraded concept needs to begin with a series of "town hall" meetings. In the South where I live they are called "ya'll come" meetings, at which parents are taught the basics of nongraded concepts including advantages, disadvantages, what the research says, and what the nongraded classroom looks like. Ask for input from parents before asking for their support.

> In order for any system to work, parents must first understand and then support it.

Once the nongraded classroom has been established, parents can be involved in a number of ways. Here are few ideas from my experience that work well.

- **Daily Journal** for students to take home and share with parents. This informal communication helps parents understand the day-to-day procedures of the classroom.
- **Monthly Calendar** with some specific reading each day for students to share with parents.
- **A Homework Kit** helps parents feel comfortable working with their child. Use an accordion folder for directions, materials, etc., for a game or activity to be done with the parents. Rotate kits throughout the classroom.

- **Student-Led Conferences** allow the child to share his or her portfolio with parents in order to create meaningful communication between school and home.
- **Parent Volunteers** are essential in a multi-age classroom. They can serve as center leaders, tutors, volunteer readers, materials gatherers, researchers, and any other roles needed by the teacher.

The value of including parents in the school is *limitless*. The ways of bringing parents into the school are *endless*, and the need to involve parents in the school is *unquestionable*. We, as educators, must make parents an essential part of the learning team.

t Works! K-1-2-3

You can do anything with children if you only play with them.
—Prince Otto Von Bismarck

Multiage, nongraded, continuous progress classrooms are often incorporated at the primary level of schooling where discovery learning is an accepted pedagogical principle. The two articles in this section are written by teachers who describe their ongoing experiences with mixed-age groupings.

Nachbar's discussion focuses on a K/1 class. This author answers the most basic but often-asked questions about implementing multiage groupings. Included are practical ways that this teacher formed cohesive groups, arranged classrooms, designed schedules and models for reading, math, and writing, and other typical classroom activities.

In the next article, Oberlander shows how the multiage, nongraded classroom can be used to bridge the developmental gap between kindergarten, first, and second graders. Instead of separating children from their peers because of a lack in certain abilities, this successful approach allows students to progress and learn from one another. In this nongraded, multiage grouping, scheduling and curriculum concerns are described, ideas for grouping students are given, and methods for the teaming of teachers are provided. A glimpse into the author's classroom demonstrates how minor scheduling adjustments and increased flexibility can create a foundation for a successful multiage program.

As is witnessed throughout the literature on nongraded, multiage, continuous progress programs, teachers who are involved in them believe in them. Many are convinced it is the only way to teach—the natural way for children's intellects and potentials to unfold.

A K/1 Class Can Work— Wonderfully!

by Randa Roen Nachbar

These are thoughts of a teacher who enjoys her K/1 class and who hopes others will ask to have a multiage group, too.

stablishing a K/1 class can create anxiety for everyone: the teacher, the principal, and the parents. (Interestingly, young children are immune!) Concerns focus on the size disparity among children, which might result in bullying; societal needs for first graders—but not kindergartners—to learn to read; and meeting the intellectual differences of children with a wider-than-usual age range. As a K/1 teacher for several years, I can report that a K/1 class can provide positive, excellent education for both kindergartners and first graders.

WHAT IS A K/1?

Our K/1 has one teacher and 25 children, on the average. According to New York state law, the kindergartners must reach age 5, and the first graders age 6, by December 31. We eagerly work together as a group, and as individuals, with very little differentiation between the grade levels. Because of their limited school experience, the children are not surprised by the age range in the classroom. Many preschools have mixed-aged classes, and, at home, siblings provide variations in age. To visitors, our room appears like any other exclusively kindergarten or first grade open classroom.

WHY ARRANGE A K/1?

Every year, the school organization changes due to fluctuations in enrollment and funding. The principal determines classes to

From *Young Children*, vol. 44, no. 5, p. 67–71,1989. Reprinted with permission.

achieve the best possible child-teacher ratio. Quite often an overflow of children on certain grade levels occurs, and the principal arranges a mixed-grade class to accommodate this overflow.

Small class size is the main practical reason to establish multiage grouping, but other benefits exist: Teachers are better able to provide individualized attention because: 1) older children are familiar with the system and need less guidance at the beginning of the year; 2) staff is familiar with the children; 3) children can help each other, which fosters the young children's socialization into the academic setting and the older children's leadership ability (Day & Hunt, 1975).

Within a K/1 class, children can naturally proceed at their own pace among their peers and not stand out as late bloomers or overachievers.

Most teachers avoid mixed classes, but I request them. I enjoy the opportunity to work with children of various ages and abilities. I find watching the children interact fascinating. Within a K/1 class, children can naturally proceed at their own pace among their peers and not stand out as late bloomers or overachievers. In essence, I see little difference between teaching an exclusively kindergarten or first grade class and teaching a mixed group. I remember feeling comfortable in a mixed-age class when I was in elementary school, and, as a teacher, I want to pass along that positive experience to my students.

WHICH CHILDREN ARE ASSIGNED TO THE K/1?

How children are chosen is an important consideration when arranging classes. Depending on the reason for the class, placement can be based on age (older 5s and younger 6s), academic ability, or maturity. My experience suggests that random selection works as well as any fixed criteria. An objective criterion (birthdate) is more readily acceptable to parents than subjective means (academic ability or maturity) as the determining factor. Parents always deserve an explanation of why their child is in a mixed-age class. Whatever the selection process, it is important that the rationale create a cooperative, not competitive, environment.

Children remain in their mixed-age class for one school year at P.S. 11. In other schools, children remain with their teacher for two school years, adding a half-class of new students (younger grade) each year. In the 2-year arrangement teachers and children benefit from the continuity with peers, materials, and procedures.

HOW DO WE FORM A COHESIVE GROUP?

Some people assume that with a wide age range the group would not be cohesive. I avoid this issue from the start by expecting all the children to collaborate as a self-contained class. The first day begins with activities to learn about each other. "Who stole the cookie from the cookie jar?" is a great icebreaker and provides practice for learning classmates' names. To emphasize our similarities, we share our common experiences and knowledge. The loss of a baby tooth is avidly discussed by the veteran and the anticipator. I do not refer to the children by grade level or age, just as I do not differentiate between the sexes. For example, the children line up with weekly rotating partners—kindergartners, first graders, boy, and girls.

All the children are new to my classroom in September, and many are new to the school. Together they learn our routines and help create our rules. The children naturally compare this situation to where they were last year; with another teacher at the school, at a preschool, or at home. It is helpful to have the "experienced" students to assist the newcomers with adjustment to school.

One ritual that promotes community feeling is the celebration of each child's birthday. Our practice has evolved to include a snack (provided by the child's family), a song, and a hug from the teacher. Family members and siblings are strongly encouraged to attend. As a memento of this special day, the class produces a birthday book, with a page contributed by each classmate, for the birthday child to take home. "Happy Birthday" are often the first words my children can read and spell. While acknowledging an age change, we focus on this as a special day. Occasionally, when some kindergartners turn 6, they insist they are now in first grade. I try to explain patiently. Summer birthdays are celebrated at half-birthday dates so that everyone gets a turn.

HOW IS THE CLASSROOM ARRANGED?

Our space resembles any active open classroom, featuring learning centers around the room: block, table toys, art, math, writing, listening, pretend, book, and puzzle areas. The corner rug doubles as the block building area and as a whole-class meeting area. The small alley to the bathroom changes function throughout the year; for example, it has been a puppet theater, a grocery store, and a Lego™ station.

Actually many learning centers are in flux throughout the school year and sometimes they even move sites. One year, the pretend area was discretely placed in the alley and changed according to curriculum themes (post office, hospital, grocery store). The next year, small groups met in the alley because children were easily distracted in the main room. The pretend area was moved to a larger, more prominent location because of its popularity. The art area, however, remains next to the sink.

When new materials appear, the children participate in deciding the name and placement of the objects. Creating a title (such as *go-together blocks*) for unusual materials is an imaginative, fun task. One year, after a heated discussion in a group meeting, voting determined that the dolls should be in the pretend, not the table toys, area. The two cash registers were split between two areas. What clever ideas children have!

Tables are grouped together (3 to 6 seats per group), so every child can have a seat. No chairs are assigned; the children are encouraged to mingle. Each child has a built-in cubby, with her or his name prominently displayed, for materials. The wardrobe closet holds our outer garments. Children's writing and drawing decorate the walls. Because we are lucky to have access to a roof-top playground, a lane must be left clear to that door.

If the door were not labeled K/1, could anyone tell we were a mixed-grade class? I doubt it.

WHAT IS OUR CURRICULUM?

So, what do children learn in this K/1 class? Socialization, cooperation, responsibility, and self-motivation are the underlying themes. Oral, written, and creative communication are emphasized. The pleasure of books, manipulations of objects, and exploration of the physical world are encouraged. Children of these transitional years need stimulation and guidance in their classrooms.

We explore curriculum through units that change every few months according to the children's interests and my whims.

The New York City Board of Education Guidelines are a resource for curriculum development. Units we tackle are common to our grade levels: the human body, food, transportation, and animals.

My favorite unit, to date, is "Exploring Our School." The children's enthusiasm to explore their school building was infectious. To begin, they listed what they knew about P.S. 11 and what the staff does. Next, the children thought about what they wanted to learn. This process directed the tour and interview arrangements.

> We explore curriculum through units that change every few months according to the children's interests and my whims.

Before conducting interviews or visits, the class discussed possible questions and interests. The visit to the "dungeon" (children's name for our mysterious basement) began with a chart of predictions: "What will we see?" On our return, we read the chart and crossed off what was not there. We called on the lunch duty teachers in their classrooms because they were seen only in the cafeteria. We visited two children's grandmothers who worked in our building, inspected their offices, and asked about their daily tasks. The popular custodian, who cheerfully collects our trash daily, reluctantly agreed to be interviewed. His plea for cooperation led to a cleaner classroom. The principal, in his office, fielded difficult questions such as "What do you do all day?" and "What makes the loudspeaker work?"

The unit culminated in a display at the school's Family Night. Each child contributed at his or her own ability level. We had lots of drawings from the nonwriters, and words and pictures from the writers. All class members added ideas to the lists and charts. The children were proud to teach others what they had learned about their school.

WHAT ABOUT THE FIRST GRADERS? WHEN DO THEY LEARN TO READ?

First graders are very anxious to learn to read. After evaluating each student's skills, I form one or more small groups for reading activities. We meet daily, during work time, for 15 to 30 minutes to practice basic reading skills. As the year progresses, I assign independent work. The first graders do reading homework nightly. For a child who stands out far ahead of the others,

I coordinate with another teacher who has students on similar reading levels. A real plus in a K/1 situation is that the first graders do not feel as much academic peer pressure because non-readers are in their class.

By January, the kindergartners are eager and ready to begin formal reading activities. I form small groups to meet three times a week. We use big books, workbooks, and games to practice reading skills. The children who are able begin to read while the others do activities appropriate to their developmental level.

> **Taking attendance, counting our snacks, and designing patterns integrate math skills with common practices.**

Another major component of the reading program for both kindergarten and first grade is quiet reading time. Each day for 10 to 30 minutes (increasingly gradually during the year), the lights are shut off; we read by window light. Children choose three books to read and ponder, and maybe discuss with a friend. Quiet reading time is a marvelous sharing time; the children learn so much from each other as well as from the books. Invariably, a first grader teaches a kindergartner some words. Their excitement with reading is contagious! During quiet reading time, to share in the discovery of books and words, I have individual, weekly conferences on a rotating schedule. A very popular time of the day.

WHAT ABOUT MATH?

Mathematics is easily incorporated into daily activities. Taking attendance, counting our snacks, and designing patterns integrate math skills with common practices. The table toys include many math manipulatives such as Cuisenaire™ rods, fractional puzzles, and hundreds boards. The first graders use a workbook to practice their math skills. Sometimes, we meet during work time for lessons or assignments. The kindergartners benefit from the first graders' mathbook units. When the first graders learn to tell time and count money, both grades get a chance to play with clocks and coins. The math skill games I teach to first graders are quickly passed along to the kindergartners who are ready.

WHAT IS AN AVERAGE DAILY SCHEDULE?

The schedule as written on the blackboard daily (see box) is altered each year because the needs of different groups of children vary. Every day, while the children are with a specialist (art, library, swimming, science), I have 45 minutes to plan. Our day always includes: work time, reading groups, quiet reading, group meeting, jobs, classroom book borrowing, snack, and story. Several times a week we engage in story writing, handwriting, music, and movement. I try to make our routine familiar to the children so they can comfortably participate. Of course, I am flexible and accommodate special events such as trips and assemblies.

Work Time

Work time is an extended period (45 to 60 minutes) for children to partake in the activity(ies) of their choice. Work time begins in anticipatory silence as I show name cards (shuffled each day) for each child. The child places her or his name on a chart by the pictured area. Many areas have limits (written on the area card) due to size and/or materials. If three children have names next to the record player picture, a classmate knows to take another option as the listening area is full.

Children work at their own speed in all these areas, trading skills and experiences. Sharing across age levels abounds. It is exciting to watch one child show another how to make an incline with the blocks. The art area activities change daily. Using simple materials such as water colors, glue, clay, and magazine pictures, children spontaneously create independent and cooperative projects. If a second adult is present, this area benefits with more complex materials, greater conversation, and better cleanup.

Group Meeting

Group meeting (15 to 30 minutes) is a whole-class sharing time. Discussions extend from our current unit to a fun outdoor weekend activity to things beginning with *R*. Sometimes everyone has a chance to talk, taking turns around the circle, and other times children raise their hands. Also, the children learn and practice new games such as "I Spy."

Writing

For story writing, three times weekly, every child has a colorful folder. I use the writing process approach, encouraging the children to compose creatively, in words and pictures, from their own experiences. To share the stories, a "guest author" presents to the whole class. The listeners ask questions or make comments about their peer's tale. Children are required to sound out or guess at word spellings so they will become fluent, confident writers. The children assist each other with story ideas as well as with spelling.

Our Daily Schedule	
8:45 - 9:15	Quiet Reading
9:15 - 9:30	Group Meeting
9:30 - 10:30	Work Time
10:30 - 11:00	Storywriting/Music/Movement
11:00 - 11:30	Lunch
11:30 - 12:00	Recess
12:00 - 12:30	Story
12:30 - 1:30	Work Time
1:30 - 2:15	Special Activity (Art, Gym, Library, Computer, Science)
2:15 - 2:30	Snack
2:30 - 2:45	Book Borrowing/Jobs
2:45 - 3:00	Dismissal

Additional Activities

Other classroom activities include handwriting, a time to practice formally printing letters on wide-lined paper. Music combines written lyrics on large charts, songs, instruments, and records. Movement encompasses aerobic exercise, folk dancing, and cooperative games.

Other daily tasks meet our curriculum goals. Classroom book borrowing affords children the opportunity to carry home their enthusiasm for stories. Snack gives the children time to converse freely, practicing their verbal skills. At the end of the day, each child has a job that changes weekly. Jobs demonstrate that we are all responsible for our room. All classmates participate, and the pleasures and results of cooperation are evident.

ARE THE KINDERGARTNERS AND FIRST GRADERS EVER DIFFERENTIATED?

Outside of formal reading and math groups, rarely do I concentrate on one grade level. Standardized testing of the first grades is required, so I prepare them a few days before. My kindergartners have a joint year-end school party with the other P.S. 11 kindergartners. As for paperwork, the report cards are different for the two grades. Taking attendance requires extra time because the grades are checked separately. Otherwise, the children and I do not pay attention to the grade designations.

ARE K/1s WORKABLE?

From my viewpoint a K/1 is delightfully workable. My principal is satisfied too as the children's academic skills are comparable to those of their schoolmates in exclusive-grade classes. Their cooperation, socialization, and motivation are probably better. Parents' beginning anxieties are invariably soothed as the year progresses. I believe that extending solid early childhood principles into first grade (rather than pushing down elementary school principles into the kindergarten) enables a successful experience for all.

FOR FURTHER READING

Chenfield, M. B. (1983). *Creative activities for young children.* New York: Harcourt Brace Jovanovich.

Cohen, D. (1972). *The learning child.* New York: Pantheon.

Hendrick, J. (1980). *Total learning for the whole child.* St. Louis: Mosby.

Ramsey, P. (1987). *Teaching and learning in a diverse world.* New York: Teachers College Press, Columbia University.

Roopnarine, J., & Johnson, J. (1983). Kindergartners' play with preschool and school aged children within a mixed-age classroom. *Elementary School Journal, 83*, 578-586.

Roopnarine, J., & Johnson, J. (1984). Socialization in a mixed-age experimental program. *Developmental Psychology, 20*, 828-832.

Seefeldt, C. (1987). *Early childhood curriculum: A review of current research.* New York: Teachers College Press, Columbia University.

REFERENCE

Day, B., & Hunt, G. (1975). Multiage classrooms: An analysis of verbal communication. *Elementary School Journal, 75,* 458-466.

A Nongraded, Multi-Aged Program That Works

by T. Marjorie Oberlander

Here's how an approach borrowed from the one-room school helps bridge the development gap between kindergarten and second grade.

In the spring of 1987 the principal and some of the teachers at John Campbell School got together in an attempt to find a realistic way to bridge the developmental gap between the kindergarten and first grade without holding children back a full year. We discussed several ideas, including transition rooms, but all of them involved separating children from their peers, which we were reluctant to do.

We wanted to develop a plan where youngsters could learn in heterogeneous groupings and still have the time necessary to master the curriculum. Eventually the discussion produced an intriguing suggestion: What would happen if we mixed five-, six-, and seven-year-olds in one class, like they did in the old one-room schools? Could we successfully mix these ages, along with a few eight-year-olds, and have the same teacher teach them—for up to four years if necessary—until they mastered the second-grade curriculum?

The more we talked in subsequent meetings about developing such a nongraded, multi-aged program, the greater the enthusiasm grew. Finally, five experienced teachers volunteered to try it during the 1987-1988 school year. All of them had taught first grade, and most had also taught kindergarten and second grade. One was a reading specialist, two were trained in early childhood education, and two had taught in multi-aged settings before. They were very eager and I was confident that

From *Principal*, vol. 68, no. 5, p. 29–30, May 1989. Reprinted with permission.

they could make the program work even though we had no extra funding and no model to follow.

We found an open area large enough for five classes, which was advantageous for planning and visual contact among the teachers. The plan was to assign each teacher approximately 30 children from five to eight years old. The children in these multi-aged groups would stay together with the same teachers until they mastered second-grade skills and moved into third-grade classrooms.

In order to assure that each group had a normal heterogeneous mix, we assigned children who were perceived as high, medium, and low in each class. We also made sure that each teacher received some children in need of special education, some minority children, and a mix of boys and girls. If parents requested that their youngster be in the program, we tried to accommodate them—if it didn't unbalance the heterogeneous mix. We did not put any students in the program whose parents did not want them there.

> In order to assure that each group had a normal heterogeneous mix, we assigned children who were perceived as high, medium, and low in each class.

The kindergartners posed the most difficult scheduling problems. In our half-day program, one of the teachers had taught about 25 kindergartners in the morning and 25 in the afternoon. To integrate these children into the new program, we decided that all of them would attend in the morning. In that way we could start the day with approximately 50 kindergartners, 50 first graders, and 50 second graders divided among five teachers. Each teacher would have about 30 multi-aged students—ten from each grade—until late morning, when the five-year-olds would leave. Each teacher would then finish the day with approximately 20 older children.

Another problem we faced was some initial skepticism from the music, physical education, and library specialists about teaching a multi-aged group of youngsters. Although we had little difficulty in adjusting music and library instruction, we were a bit concerned about the developmental aspects of physical education. Early in the year the teachers worked with the physical education specialist to analyze children's physical skills before regrouping them into different physical skills groups. For

Campbell School's Nongraded Schedule

8:15 - 8:30	Opening and calendar
8:30 - 8:40	Silent sustained reading
8:40 - 9:20	Language experience and centers
9:20 - 9:55	Special classes
9:55 - 10:10	Recess
10:10 - 10:55	Centers (integrated subjects)
10:55	Dismissal, half-day children
10:55 - 11:55	Math
11:55 - 12:45	Lunch
12:45 - 1:00	Story reading by teacher
1:00 - 2:00	Reading
2:20	Dismissal

30 minutes each day, one of these groups would go to P.E., two to music (different teachers), one to the library, and one to a class in personal safety and drug and alcohol awareness. The arrangement worked well.

In order to teach children of different age and developmental levels, the teachers have created a concrete, hands-on environment where children are actively involved. They use a whole-language approach to reading, writing, and spelling. Social studies and science are integrated into special teaching centers, with units rotated each year to avoid repetition.

The whole-language approach incorporates speaking, listening, chanting, singing, writing, and spelling in many different settings. Children learn the rhythm of language and how it is structured. The teachers have found that the six- and seven-year-olds can read more difficult books and can write whole stories while the five-year-olds dictate stories or look up words in a book.

Because multi-aged children cooperate and learn from one another, the teachers feel that they have been able to meet most students' needs at appropriate levels without resorting to ability groups.

Now in its second year, our program has been successful because it provides a developmentally appropriate environment for young children without rejection or separation from peers. If a child needs additional time to learn certain skills, it can be provided in a comfortable, familiar setting. The program can be tailored to their needs and achievement and it includes lots of teacher/student interaction, hands-on experiences, cooperative learning, peer tutoring, and an integrated approach to learning—all elements recommended for young children by the National Association for the Education of Young Children.

I hope other administrators will see the advantaged of this approach and look for creative ways they might apply the same concept to their early childhood programs.

M odels for Intermediate Levels

What we want most is to see the child in pursuit of knowledge, and not knowledge in pursuit of the child.—George Bernard Shaw

While nongraded, multiage classrooms seem to appear more frequently at the primary levels, there are viable models in our schools that demonstrate the successes and benefits of multiage groupings at the upper levels as well. This section profiles four quite different approaches to this concept. One is a third-fourth combination class, another is a four-five integrated technology classroom, a third compares multigrade and single grade classrooms, and yet a fourth is a classroom consensus model for 11, 12, and 13 year olds. Each has a unique concept that guides the structure and content of schooling.

Freeman discovers the unexpected benefits and pleasures of teaching a combined third and fourth grade class. The author enlightens readers with the logistics of her multiage classroom such as decisions that were made about teaching one or two separate curricula, organizational schemes, and parental concerns. Her analysis ends with a comparison of her classroom to the family and the rewards that accompany that special grouping.

The "Integrated Technology Classroom," on the other hand, delineates the teaming of two 4/5 grade teachers with curriculum and technology specialists to restructure a classroom-based model of computer technology. They talk about moving from a "sage on the stage" posture to adopting a "guide on the side" philosophy in which cooperative learning takes on a major role in their classroom. In fact, they describe computers as "aides" as they progress, through each year, from more structured approaches at learning stations, to a more open-ended, problem-solving workshop atmosphere by the end of the term.

In a third piece, Brown and Martin compare achievement in multigrade to single grade classes. While test scores favored the multiage classroom, and teachers and principals favored teaching in the mixed-age groupings, the grade points awarded students were not significantly different.

Finally, in the consensus classroom, Sartor and Sutherland describe a classroom of 11, 12 and 13 year olds using daily meetings to set agendas based on student interest and priorities. In this piece, the self-examination of the process is enlightening to read as the vision of the consensus classroom evolves.

How I Learned to Stop Worrying and Love My Combination Class

by Jayne Freeman

One teacher's discovery of the unexpected benefits and pleasures of teaching a combined third and fourth grade class.

At the beginning of the year, Jeff, a bright third grader, was functioning at the fourth grade level academically but not socially. Now he is continuing to read and do math at the fourth grade level and has lost most of his immature ways. Brian, a fourth grader, had been considered for retention in the third grade because of his immaturity and slow progress in reading, spelling, and math. In my class he has been able to work at the third-grade level in these subjects without feeling stigmatized—others are at that level, too. Angela is a mainstreamed student of fifth grade age who reads at the primer level and odes third-grade-level math. In this class she doesn't stand out as being as different from the others as she would in a regular fourth grade classroom. Other children function close to where she is.

There are just three reasons why the apprehension I felt in September about teaching 16 fourth graders and 9 third graders in a combined class proved to be needless. What started out as an expedient measure to accommodate a declining enrollment has turned out to be positively beneficial for all concerned. If you are planning to teach a multigrade class yourself, take some hints from my own experience—you're in for a rewarding year.

The chances that you *will* be faced with a combination class someday are better than ever, as declining enrollments make

From *Instructor*, vol. 93, no. 7, p. 48–54, March 1984. Reprinted with permission.

split-level classes more and more widespread. But teachers who have taught such classes are also beginning to initiate them even when the enrollment is not declining. They have discovered that combined classes can provide greater flexibility in classroom organization, more individualized instruction, and the opportunities to group children according to ability, rather than grade level and to use cross-age tutoring.

In my own class, I have watched the strengths of each group spill over into the other. The fourth graders' artwork, for example, at first small and inhibited as is sometimes common with this age, is becoming more imaginative, more like the bold, confident, and colorful drawings of the third graders. The babyish ways of the third graders are nearly gone as they imitate their older models; their attention spans have grown, and their tendency to tattle has shrunk.

My students are coming to think of themselves as multilevel people who need help with some things and are able to give help with others. When Charline wants to write in her journal but can't spell the words, one of her classmates will help her. Charline, who is a good artist, may help that student later on with art. There are academic benefits, too: a recent study by Dennis Milburn, a professor at the University of British Columbia, showed that students in the lower grade level in a combined class achieve above grade level, those in the higher grade achieve at or above grade level, and the entire group has a greater liking for school.

> My students have begun to think of themselves as multilevel people who need help with some things and who are able to give help with others.

When I was first planning for my new class, I decided not to make my seating chart according to grade level, but to mix the grades together. I wanted to give the more able children a chance to share their skills regardless of grade level, and I wanted my group to develop class spirit and solidarity. The second week of school, I rearranged seats based on student requests. Of nine third graders, a group of four asked to sit together. The others had made fourth grade friends. Now, halfway through the year, students' friendships are entirely cross-grade and are based on such solid reasons for making friends as common interests and maturity level, rather than age or grade.

One of the challenges posed by combined classes is that of planning and teaching two separate curriculums. If you are used to forming groups for reading and math, these subjects will be relatively easy to handle. For others, like handwriting, language arts, health, science, and social studies, my advice is to find common areas within each subject as starting-off points. In my class, for instance, each health book has a unit on nutrition. I presented this topic to the whole class through discussion, demonstration, and films. Students all charted what they ate for breakfast and learned about the four food groups together. They then used their grade-level texts for additional study and special projects.

I did something similar with poetry. We shared the poems in both third and fourth grade language books as a group: third graders read poems from their books to the class and fourth graders read aloud from theirs. Each group had to listen carefully, making the experience of poetry an oral activity, as it should be. Then I worked with third graders to write a group poem as described in the teacher's guide, while the fourth graders worked independently on a poetry-writing assignment in their texts. It was not too different from assigning seat work to one reading group while meeting with another.

Reading can be a special problem. Unless students are handpicked for grade-level skills, there will be a greater span of skill levels than in a single-grade class. My students range from second to sixth grade in reading ability; I have five reading groups. I meet with three each day, all of them every two days. While I meet with a group, the other children work on reading, journal writing, handwriting practice, and spelling, and anyone who needs help may consult one of my "student teachers." These are two or three students I have picked for their skills in reading or spelling; I choose new ones from time to time to give all the able children a chance to be a helper. It is a coveted position in the room, and includes both third and fourth graders.

In my school, students go as a class to P.E. and music, leaving those half hours free to teachers for valuable planning time. I way afraid my new class would deprive me of that planning time, with each grade going separately to those classes. But when I asked the P.E. and music teachers how they felt about teaching my class as a whole, they both liked the idea. The librarian, however, thought her particular series of lessons in library skills were too different in third and fourth grades, so we agreed she would take my class by grade level for their month of library skill lessons. This gave me useful time of grade-level instruction with each grade alone.

There are different ways of organizing a combination class. June Smythe, another teacher in my district who teaches a third, fourth, and fifth grade class of students with learning and behavior problems, uses her combination class to teach in an almost completely individualized way. She encourages children to work independently and take on responsibility for their own time by means of monthly assignment sheets. At the beginning of each month, June issues each child two copies of the assignment sheet. One copy goes home to parents so they can help the child at home; the other stays with the child, who checks off work as it is completed. Some assignments are for the whole class, some are for each grade level, and some are for a particular individual.

> **However you decide to organize your combination class, inform parents of your methods or teaching goals before the year begins.**

Each morning, June's students begin by listing their daily assignments in order of importance. June asks them to ask themselves, "What does the teacher feel I need to do most?" to eliminate the temptation to do the easiest ones first, and to consider which assignments they must complete at school and which can be taken home if necessary. Students also plan for themselves what they will do if they have extra time during the day. June defines extra time as either "free time" (art activities, playing chess, reading a library book, or a similar activity) or "open time" (spent on supplemental academic work). She tells children before a work period whether finishing early will involve free or open time, and asks them to be aware of areas they should be working on during open time (handwriting, spelling, multiplication facts).

This method seems to work smoothly in her class. Children who finish early with one assignments go on independently to another or work on practice activities. They also go in small groups during the day to special subjects like P.E., Chapter I reading, or math, while June carries on with the groups that remain in the class.

However you decide to organize your combination class, inform parents of your methods or teaching goals before the year begins. Last September I was told that two parents had requested their children be transferred from my class into the other fourth grade class. I discovered later that they and other parents had felt their children could not learn as much as they would in a single-grade class. This situation could be avoided by arranging a parent meeting the week before school. Explain how you can meet the needs of all students, accelerated, average, or remedial, and that you intend to approach each child as an individual with strengths and weaknesses, regardless of the grade-level label of the class unit. You might also mention the positive results, in both academic and social areas, that have been found in recent studies on the effectiveness of multigrade classes.

Now when parents or anyone else ask me what it's like teaching a split class, I generally answer that it's not that different from teaching a regular class, Your students are yours to help every year, and you deal with whatever academic, social, or emotional needs they may have. I have talked to many teachers of combined classes during the past few months, and several told me they now always ask for a split class. They have come to know firsthand the atmosphere of closeness and cooperation that a combined class can have. "The class became like a family, helping one another," commented one teacher. "I like to see kids accept the fact that they can be third-grade level in one area and fifth-grade in another, and it's okay," said another. It's a special situation, and the rewards are just as special.

The Integrated Technology Classroom

An Experiment in Restructuring Elementary School Instruction

by Chris Held, John Newsom, and Marian Peiffer

How can we best prepare students for the Information Age and the developing planetary culture? How can the needs of all students be met in a heterogeneous classroom? How can technology be integrated into new methods of instruction? How much technology is needed for effective use by students and teachers? When creative and dedicated teachers sit down to discuss interesting questions, the results often mean change and improvement.

In Washington State's Bellevue School District, we began to explore these questions in the winter of 1988. Grade 4/5 teachers Chris Held and Marian Peiffer met with curriculum specialist Nancy Place and district technology coordinator John Newsom to develop what would become the Integrated Technology Classroom (ITC) project. During the months we planned and discussed, clear images of a shared vision emerged. We all believed that preparing students for the future meant that students needed to be life-long learners, excited about learning, and self directed. Students should have frequent opportunities to interact with computers and possibly other technology as part of their everyday lives and work. Students would be expected to work cooperatively and actively, constructing their own meaning and knowledge from the tasks they were involved in. We assumed a classroom-based rather

> **We all believed that preparing students for the future meant that students needed to be life-long learners, excited about learning, and self directed.**

From *The Computing Teacher*, vol. 18, no. 6, p. 21–23, March 1991. Reprinted with permission.

than lab model for computer use, and pictured computers becoming tools in a learning environment that focused on problem solving mathematics, whole language opportunities, and integrated curriculum.

District-wide curriculum initiatives needed to support these ideas were already in progress. Five years before, committees of teachers, administrators, and parents had begun creating a shared vision of elementary education. During this time the district had implemented extensive inservice programs in Marilyn Burns' "Math Solution," cooperative learning, GEESA (Gender/Ethnic Expectations, Student Achievement), and whole language.

It is safe to say that the integrated approach to using technology imagined by Chris, Marian, John, and Nancy could not work independent of these other, systemic changes. To place eight computers, a camcorder, a CD-ROM player, a videodisc player, a VCR, and other peripheral equipment in a classroom and expect change is naive. If the supporting structures in curriculum and practice mentioned above are not in place, if the teacher has not learned how to apply cooperative learning strategies, if the teacher is not comfortable giving up control from the front of the classroom, if curriculum is narrowly defined as content coverage—then all the fancy technology is a waste of money. But if these key elements are present, the impact of the technology can be impressive, and energizing for both student and teacher. In fact, one of the most important things this project has pointed out is the critical need for the teacher to develop a *personal* vision of instruction—to take the elements of curriculum, practice, technology, and interest and build his or her own model for their classroom, rather than following a detailed recipe—to truly be a composer of the learning environment, instead of a musician reading and interpreting someone else's score.

One other key element of integrating technology into the classroom is having a multi-aged grouping of students. Having two grades in the same class has two definite advantages: 1) the teacher has the students for two years, thus having more time to get to know them; and 2) the returning upper grade students act as peer tutors for the incoming lower grade students, transferring their operational knowledge of the technology in the classroom, and freeing the teacher from that task. The multi-aged classroom works best if the teacher only teaches one curriculum, not two or more. For this reason, most elementary schools in Bellevue run a rotating cycle of science and social studies curricula, teaching all fourth and fifth graders U.S. history one year, and world geography the next.

What is it like to teach in this restructured environment? What were some of the inspirations to take the road less traveled? What do these classrooms look like, and how do they work? Chris and Marion will outline their answers to these questions below.

DEVELOPMENT OF VISION

Chris: A major piece of the restructuring puzzle fell into place by accident for me. When I brought that first computer into the classroom I was faced with a problem. Since the kids couldn't all work on the computer at once, I realized that this was going to infringe on my whole-class teacher lecture method! The solution was to leave my "Sage on the Stage" posture, move to a learning centers approach that had technology in one or two of the centers, and adopt a "Guide on the Side" philosophy that allowed kids to work more independently and allowed me to move about the room working with small groups of children.

> Some wonderful things happened as a result of the initial restructuring of the classroom into centers.

Some wonderful things happened as a result of the initial restructuring of the classroom into centers. I found that the technology centers functioned far better than the centers I had tried years earlier. The computer was a source of constant, non-judgmental feedback for the children and that made my intervention much less necessary. This allows me to focus on other centers and not feel guilty that some kids weren't getting the feedback they needed and I was not having to work any harder than I was when the room was "Teacher Centered." The computers were actually serving as my "aides."

Another discovery born of necessity was that two are better than one. By that I mean two kids on a computer are almost always better than one alone. At first I decreed two to a computer because I had so few computers and wanted to spread out a limited resource. Lo and behold, there were other benefits with two on a computer. Students talked to each other, they problem-solved, and they shared duties. Since then I have learned more about the work of Johnson and Johnson on cooperative learning. I have come to realize what a nice tool a computer is in this very important world of cooperative learning.

Marian: A paradigm shift in my vision for education and the elementary classroom simmered for years as I took time out from my profession and raised my children. Watching my two children grow and thrive in unconventional classrooms brought Piaget's constructivist theories to reality for me.

Upon re-entering the classroom world myself five years ago, I was determined to find ways to create a classroom where all students were excited about learning, involved in setting their own goals for learning, and actively constructing meaning from the learning. This proved to be much easier said than done! The hands-on, interactive materials that were so plentiful at the primary levels were not available or effective at the intermediate level. I was determine to move away from whole-group teaching in order to actively involve the wide range of children in the multi-age group I was teaching.

My work with remedial math and my interest in computers, which had developed during my years away from full time teaching, gradually emerged as an effective beginning for change. Once a week, I borrowed two computers and set up math stations. I used the computers at two stations, math manipulatives at two others, and direct instruction at another. The student involvement level and interaction were exciting. At that time, math programs were largely drill and practice, so I began to use Logo to fill in the critical piece of problem solving in mathematics. The excitement soared as students "discovered" how to make elaborate geometrical designs, create polygons, and animate graphics, I was hooked!

I wrote a grant to have two computers in my room and began the process of undoing my classroom structures so I could take advantage of those two machines effectively. Gradually, I tried new groupings, more interaction, less whole group direct teaching. I could sense the attitude of self confidence grow as students became more independent.

A year later, when John, Chris, and Nancy asked me to join them in what has become the ITC project and a continuing saga of change and exploration, I was eager to go further. As more equipment became available, the process of change accelerated. Changing schedules, moving furniture, and creating new types of activities became an ongoing process as Chris and I, supported by John and Nancy, created a new paradigm for our classrooms.

ELEMENTS OF AN INTEGRATED TECHNOLOGY CLASSROOM

Chris: When Marian and I began our ITC experiment four years ago, we had one computer for each group of four children. The initial goal was to insure that each child had several computer experiences each day where the computer was the tool that helped the child get about the business of learning.

Right from the beginning, the backbone of our rooms has been Logo. It is such an open-ended, mathematically rich, problem solving oriented, easily integrated program that it has maintained that "backbone" status in both our rooms. Other software programs and other technologies are also centerpieces of our classroom environments because they all have one thing in common. They provide a tool that is better for learning than the old-fashioned pencil, paper, and textbook. Some of those improvements include: LEGO/Logo for part of our science curriculum, laptop computers for our writing in language arts, a camcorder for student projects and presentations, Macintoshes for publishing of children's stories and the "creme de la creme" problem solving software from companies such as Sunburst and MECC.

Marian: Some standard pieces emerged as critical and are still a part of our classroom environment today. Logo is a key piece in the environment, providing opportunities for students to explore microworlds in mathematics while giving us windows into their thinking processes as we observe their work. Math problem solving software supports the broader scope of the mathematic curriculum recommended for the 21st century: logical thinking, visual spatial thinking, number sense, pattern and function, and probability. Word processing became possible on a regular basis as soon as we had one computer for every four students. This opened new worlds for the writing and publishing process. A new microworld for Logo, LEGO/Logo, was announced, and we quickly became a part of that culture, allowing students to explore physics, design, and robotics through their work with LEGOs and Logo programming.

THE FLOW OF INSTRUCTION

Marian: We have discovered that there seems to be a flow to each year. The fall begins with more structured approaches and more specific tasks and is usually organized around centers or stations where new skills can be learned and cooperative learning strategies can be practiced. Gradually during the year, students become more independent, more confident with equipment and more involved in ongoing projects that they create. Students who have been in the program previous years, quickly help new students catch on to the system and the skills.

As the year progresses, students become more independent and projects become more open ended. Students determine more of the direction to their learning and then share their own learning with others through discussion, media, presentations, and so forth. Basic skills are woven into the fabric of the day through both teacher requirements and suggestions and through individual student interest. By the end of the year, there is a true "workshop" atmosphere as students and teacher work side by side to develop and create learning together. The schedules and assignments become open-ended and flow as needed for the community of learners. Students are problem solvers who work cooperatively and independently to achieve goals they have set. Each year the progress becomes more evident as we become more skilled at creating the environment and providing the assistance. The classroom culture becomes richer as "old timers" share their knowledge and skills with "newcomers."

> Students determine more of the direction to their learning and then share their own learning with others through discussion.

Chris: For the past two years, all my students stay in the classroom. If they need special help, that help comes to them. In an activity-based, non-teacher-centered room, the coming and going of special teachers is a little-noticed occurrence. They come in and work with the kids who need their help. They help them with classroom assignments and projects that those kids are already involved with. They don't give extra assignments. They don't pull kids away, because they know it disrupts continuity and accountability.

DISSEMINATION OF THE PROJECT

During the second year of the ITC project, the project leaders reached out to others who wanted to join this exciting adventure. A rigorous application form was developed so that interested teachers could get on board. That year, four new classrooms were added. The pace was accelerated even further last year as 17 new classrooms joined the project, and this year, 23 more. It is important to note that the teachers who sign up to "create" their own integrated technology classroom do so voluntarily, and receive the equipment with the understanding that extra work will be involved, including training and leadership responsibilities in their own schools. At this time, there are over 50 integrated technology classrooms operating with third through sixth grade students, affecting approximately 1,500 of the 5,000 students in those grade levels. The goal over the next four years is to expand the project to all third, fourth, fifth, sixth, and seventh graders.

THE FUTURE

The ITC project is committed to the idea that the "Classroom of the Future" is a moving target. Each year, new technologies, new research findings, and new practices will promote continued change. Professional development through conferences and classes seed new ideas into teacher's minds. Multimedia, increased use of community experiences, telecommunication, and electronically enhanced research are some of the concepts under exploration this year. After that, a new horizon beckons.

Student Achievement in Multigrade and Single Grade Classes

by Kenneth G. Brown and Andrew B. Martin

Which is better? A recent New Brunswick study finds that from the standpoint of overall grades there are no significant differences in achievement between these two types of classrooms.

Are there differences in achievement between multigrade classes and the traditional single grade classes? There is considerable controversy in New Brunswick about the effects of multigrade classes on the achievement of children in the elementary school. As schools experience declines in enrollment, there are occasions when there are not enough pupils to permit single grade classes. This means that more schools are establishing classes that combine two grades.

In smaller schools, multigrade classes seem likely to increase as administrators are forced to maintain pupil-teacher ratios. Larger enrollments in city areas have meant there are enough children to continue the individual grade tradition. The little red schoolhouse of days gone by had all the pupils in one classroom and the current reductions in the school population indicate a partial return to multigrade classrooms.

The integration concept of having handicapped students in a regular classroom is similar to a multigrade situation since different levels of students are grouped for instruction given by a single teacher. It may well be that the claimed advantages and disadvantages of integration will also be found in a multigrade class.

A comprehensive examination of multigrade classrooms in Saskatchewan[1] concluded that the numbers of these classes

From *Education Canada*, p. 10–13, 47, Summer 1989. Reprinted with permission.

were increasing primarily because of lower enrollment. In many schools, those teachers with the least seniority had little choice but to teach multigrade classes. Insufficient time for planning, teaching and marking in multigrade settings was reported and as principals recommended the development of special multigrade curricula, teachers were reported to be active in the search for successful teaching strategies.

> Almost all authors writing about the topic are enthusiastic about the multigrade class.

A summary report by Acheson[2] claimed that parents and teachers do not approve of multigrade classes. His survey consistently reported equal or superior achievement compared to single grade students, but no reasons were given to explain any differences. The claim that multigrading increases social and personal adjustment has not been supported.[3] Very little research has been done on cognitive development between the two class types.

Almost all authors writing about the topic are enthusiastic about the multigrade class. Such claims as superior academic achievement, enabling students to work at their own level in subjects, and the dissolving of barriers of age and grade attitudes occur often.[4] However, a comprehensive study by Finley and Thompson,[5] who carefully matched students in 28 schools with multigrade classes to those in 23 single grade schools, concluded there were no significant differences between the groups in reading or arithmetic skills as measured by the California Achievement Battery, form W. The authors have also presented criticisms or four studies favouring multigrading and four studies that found no differences between multi and single grade classes.

At the same time, Massey and Crosley[6] emphasized that teachers need to be prepared to meet multi-level classes in a rural setting, as this is the norm. Perhaps the cycle is now complete in many rural settings and the modified little red schoolhouse has come back into its own.

The samples selected in our study were from elementary schools that had regular or single grades as well as multigrades. In the spring and fall of 1985 schools were selected in five districts.

METHOD AND DATA COLLECTION

Superintendents for School Districts 9, 19, 25, 26, and 28 in New Brunswick agreed to support the study and recommended a total of eight elementary schools in their districts that had single and multigrade classes at the same grade levels. The principals of the recommended schools were contacted and arrangements made for the authors to have access to final report cards for the 1984 and 1985 school years during visits which took place between May and November 1985.

The June academic achievements of students in the selected multi-grade classes were recorded under subjects as actual percentage marks or as ratings such as "Excellent, Very Good, Good, Minimal/Fair, Not Satisfactory." In one school it was necessary to use scores recorded for the Canadian Test of Basic Skills. Each of the multigrade students was then matched to a single grade peer in the same school on the basis of sex, age and grade level. Birth-date records were used and students were matched often to the precise month. Final 1984 and 1985 report card ratings were recorded for both the selected groups.

To sample teacher and principal opinions a questionnaire was distributed to members of the schools' teaching staffs who had at some time in their careers taught multigrade classes. The questions focused on teacher preferences and work load differences between single and multigrade teaching assignments.[7]

ANALYSIS AND RESULTS

Report cards in most schools used a five category rating scale to indicate achievement in each subject: Excellent, Very Good, Good, Minimal or Fair, Not Satisfactory. Other schools had four categories or actual percentage marks. In one school, the results of the Canadian Test of Basic Skills were used to compare student achievement because the assessments were anecdotal. Whichever system of reporting achievement was used, the same applied to both groups for comparison purposes. Only the June report cards were examined for each student on the total academic year.

The values of Chi-square were calculated for six of the eight schools with similar report cards. Students in two schools with actual percentage grades were averaged over all subjects and then the grade means were compared by the 't' Test. For

Table 1
Grade Point Comparisons
for 18 Groups—Single and Multigrade

Schools	Grade Points		Class Mean	
	SG	MG	SG	MG
A, B, C, G, H	15,105	15,270		
E, F	3,683	3,743		
TOTALS	18,788	19,013	1043.78	1056.28
			"t" = .06 NS.	

MG.—Multigrade; SG.—Single-grade
NS. No significant difference

another school the results of the Canadian Test of Basic Skills were used as a criteria for comparison purposes. In this case the trend for superiority was split between grades 3 and 4.

DISCUSSION

For eight schools in five school districts, students in multigrades were matched with peers in single grades 1 to 5 inclusive. Achievement on a class by class basis was compared. From the 20 comparison groups, eleven or 55% had superior performances favouring the multigrade classes, while five or 25% were not significantly different. Only four comparisons or 20% favoured the regular class students.

When the total grade points for 18 comparison classes were averaged, there was no significant overall difference between the two classroom situations. Thus the null hypothesis is accepted and no difference between the grade points awarded each group was found.

CANADIAN TEST OF BASIC SKILLS EVALUATIONS

In addition to the teacher ratings, for 12 classes the Canadian Test of Basic Skills (CTBS) scores were obtained from five schools while the students were in their grade 4 year. They therefore do not reflect the results of being in either of the instruction situations. These scores were examined to obtain evi-

Table 2
Comparisons of Eight Classes in MG or SG Grouping
Total CTBS Scores over Four Schools

Schools	CTBS Class Scores		Class Mean		"t"
	SG	MG	SG	MG	
A, B, D, G	353.12	385.38	44.14	48.17	1.17 NS

SG—Single-grade   MG—Multigrade   NS—No Significant Difference

dence on whether or not the children in the multigrade classes were different from those in the regular classes. Discussions with principals and teachers revealed that children were selected for the multigrade classes. The criteria used were maturity, co-operation, and willingness to work with minimal supervision.

In summary, for the eight comparisons using results from CTBS scores, only one favoured the single grade, four favoured the multigrade and three were equal. These results are very similar to those based on teacher ratings and supports the conclusion that there is about an 80% chance that achievement is equal or superior to that of the single grade. When all the CTBS scores for each class are combined over all schools, the results were as shown in Table 2.

Even when CTBS achievement grades were used as the criterion, the null hypothesis was not rejected and there was no significant difference between the single and multigrade students overall.

TEACHER SURVEY
Principals and teachers were asked to answer six questions to determine their views on teaching multigrade classes. Those who answered the questions were required to have had experience in both regular and multigrade classrooms.

Of the 34 replies, the majority (29) were female teachers. Only 18% were in a multigrade class, 18% were either in special or physical educational settings, and the rest (64%) were in single-grade classes. When asked their preference for teaching, the majority (79.4%) chose the single grade. Only 3% preferred the multigrade class, while 17.6% had no preference for one or the other.

Almost all respondents stated that increased preparation time was required for multigrade classes, and there was less time in class for discussing topics compared to a single grade. Only two teachers submitted reasons why multigrade classes are superior to single grades. Finally, 26% said the workload was the same for both class types. However, the balance (74%) or almost three-quarters reported that significantly more work was required in the multigrade classroom. Not a single person felt that a lower workload was required in the multigrade classroom. Not a single person felt that a lower workload occurred in the multigrade class.

CONCLUSIONS

Evaluation of the final report card of 418 students from grades 1 to 5 inclusive in eight different schools revealed a number of conclusions.

1. There were differences in achievement between students in multigrades and their matched counterparts in single grades. However, only 20% of the comparisons favoured the single grades and 80% were equivalent to or favoured the multigrade classes. Similar findings were also found using CTBS scores as criterion (13% and 87% respectively).

2. For all schools and classes, the grade points awarded students in either class setting were not significantly different. Thus, overall, the hypothesis, namely, there is no significant difference between single and multigrade classes was supported. In comparing the total CTBS scores for the two groups which were available, there was no difference between groups.

3. From a teacher-principal questionnaire answered by 34 persons, all of whom had experience in teaching both types of class, almost 80% preferred teaching in the single grade class and 17% had no preference for one over the other.

4. Increased preparation time and less time for discussion were the major reasons why teachers preferred the single grade.

5. Almost three-quarters of the respondents claimed that significantly more work was required in the multigrade classroom while the balance (26%) felt the workload was equivalent. Not a single reply indicated a lower workload in the multigrade classroom.

6. Discussions with teachers and principals showed that the multigrade students are selected on the basis of maturity and co-operation. As long as this process of selection occurs, there is no evidence of disadvantage with respect to achievement based on evidence from this study. On a school-by-school analysis there is an 80% chance that children will perform as well or even better than their counterparts in the single grade class.

NOTES

1.   J. Gajadharsingh, "The Multigrade Classroom in Saskatchewan," *The Saskatchewan Educational Administrator*, Spring 1982, pp. 2-41.

2.   J.F. Acheson, "Memorandum on Combined Grades," Edmonton Catholic School Board, Edmonton, 22 October 1984.

3.   Bonnie E. Ford, "Multiage Grouping in the Elementary School and Children's Affective Development: A Review of Recent Research," *Elementary School Journal*, November 1977, pp. 149-159; Barbara Day and G.J. Hunt, "Multiage Classrooms: An Analysis of Verbal Communication," *Elementary School Journal*, April 1975, pp. 458-464.

4.   James Retson, "Are We Back to the Little Red Schoolhouse?", *Grade Teacher*, February 1966, pp. 108-110.

5.   C.J. Finley and J.M. Thompson, "A Comparison of Achievement of Multi-graded and Single-graded Rural Elementary School Children," *The Journal of Educational Research*, May-June 1963, pp. 471-475.

6.   S. Massey and J. Crosley, "Preparing Teachers for Rural Schools," *ERIC ED* 28-025.

7.   The teacher and principal questionnaire and its results are available from Dr. Ken Brown at the University of New Brunswick.

The Consensus Classroom

by Linda Sartor with Kate Sutherland

Making decisions as a class saves time later on.

In the consensus classroom, all decisions normally made by a teacher alone are turned over to the class as a whole. A consensus is reached when everyone agrees, including the teacher. Through this process, the group as a living organism is allowed to emerge, so no two consensus classrooms look the same. Here are descriptions of what has occurred in my classroom of 11-, 12- and 13-year-olds at Windsor Middle School, in Santa Rosa, California.

I begin at the beginning of the year. This is not essential, but there may be an advantage to getting started before everyone has established set social patterns. Because of the risk in starting something new, it is helpful to remember that students will do anything you ask on the first day. I spend the first day and a great deal of the first two weeks building a sense of community—both physically through trust activities and cooperative games, and mentally by developing a common vision out of everyone's individual goals.

> **It is helpful to remember that students will do anything you ask on the first day.**

Daily class meetings are essential from the beginning. To introduce the process, I give students a single decision to consider on the first day—What should we do for homework tonight?

I begin our first formal classroom meeting the second day by writing "Agenda" on the chalkboard and asking, "What do you want to talk about?" I write down topics they suggest. I also suggest topics if I see something I think is needed that they have not come up with. Some form of "How do we want to manage

From *Education Digest*, January 1992, p. 47–50. Reprinted with permission.

the classroom?" needs to be included. Then we must decide which topic is most important to discuss first. Sometimes, the decision of which topic is most important can be a long discussion in itself.

Usually, one of the first things students want is to elect classroom officers, which involves many decisions—what offices are needed, job descriptions for officers, terms of office, whether one can be reelected for the same office. Often, the president leads class meetings, once elected, and I sit down in one of the student desks to model full participation in the meeting.

A corner of the chalkboard is set aside for the ongoing agenda, which can be added to by anyone at any time. Some ideas, such as a judicial system (for resolving disputes and upholding agreements) are carried by word of mouth from one year to the next. Decisions such as the classroom management plan or the room arrangement change throughout the year. The source of an agenda item can be a problem someone perceives, an administrative decision I'm supposed to make, or an idea someone wants to try.

> One of the first days one year, the class and I spent two hours discussing one hour of homework. After that, no other decision took as long.

Some ideas die after an agreement is made if no one has enough energy to keep them going.

Some ideas lead to priceless learning opportunities. The class decided to do "egg babies" and experience taking care of an egg as if it were a baby. The project was originally planned as a demonstration of the tremendous responsibility of having a child, but my students were actually experiencing it more like "playing house." A parent who had given birth as a teenager called to express concern about the message students were getting. I appreciated her concern and invited her to share her story, which touched all my students very deeply; I could not have planned a lesson more valuable.

In the beginning stages of a group's consensus decision making, there invariably arises a seemingly endless discussion about a "trivial" topic. Frustration peaks in the group, and many participants are ready to give up. It is critical at this point to stay with the discussion and trust the process. At this point, it is not the content of the decision that is important but the process that the group is going through.

For example, a daily decision is what to do for homework. On one of the first days one year, we spent two hours discussing one hour of homework. After that, no other decision took as long. Students would much rather be in action than sit around a long time talking about what to do. Once a decision is made that everyone agrees with, there is 100 percent participation with no opposition draining energy from the activity. Magic happens.

The consensus classroom organically develops techniques to expedite its process. One way is actually to vote. When the decision is a selection among preferences, we list the choices on the board and look at the list to see if there is anything anyone cannot go along with. Then we vote, and the preference with the most votes is the choice. Sometimes, authority is delegated to a committee either entirely or by asking the committee to work out a recommendation which the group approves (or disapproves) by consensus.

> **Some consensus groups require that everyone says "yes." Others let members "stand aside" if not fully in favor but also not wanting to block the decision.**

Some consensus groups require that everyone says "yes." Others let members "stand aside" if not fully in favor but also not wanting to block the decision.

When it comes to different subjects, the same principle applies: Every decision I would normally make on my own I turn over to my class as a whole. Generally, we take time to decide how to learn the required curriculum material during the classroom time assigned (by the local education authority) to that subject.

As for grading homework, the first time homework was due, we brainstormed a list of criteria for evaluating it. This list was posted all year and could be added to at any time. In small groups of three to five, students share their homework and receive feedback on its strengths and weaknesses. Based on the feedback from their groups and the list of criteria, students grade themselves on their own work and give the reasons they deserve the grade. We say "C+" is average and take it from there. I agree or disagree with the grade based somewhat on my judgment of the quality of the work but more strongly based on the reason given by the student.

After two years with groups I often looked forward to spending the day with, I faced the most challenging students I'd ever had. I had previously used the consensus process with students dealt me by chance, but now my classroom's new status as a pilot alternative meant that students came with preconceptions and expectations.

I was discouraged the first day when I asked students to say why they were in the consensus classroom. The main answers were, "I thought it would be fun," or "I thought it would be easy." I had attracted students with the idea of participating in making their own decisions, and then had accepted them on a first-come, first-served basis. I now realize the importance of an application and interview process (if the consensus classroom is offered as a formal alternative) that would make each student take a serious look at the commitment and responsibility required.

The class continuously provided me with opportunities to face my personal issues. I struggle with my desire to look good, which intensified once the consensus classroom became a pilot alternative. I wanted others to think I was a "good" teacher. I wanted to look good to parents and the administration so we could continue. When I got thinking how a particular moment in class would look to an outsider walking in, the magic would be lost.

STUDENT REMINDERS

When things in class began to look out of control, I'd get scared and want to control more. At first, I'd express anger, but that frightened some of the more sensitive students who hadn't done anything to deserve the anger, and parents began to object. Then I would slip into an authority mode, dishing out consequences and hating myself for that. Often, some of the more bold students (quick to demonstrate they had learned to speak up) would remind me it was a consensus classroom.

A strong clique of girls formed that wanted to exert "power over" as opposed to the "power with" I hoped for. They interpreted my encouraging them to support each other to mean supporting each other against me or somebody else. Whenever I confronted any of them, the whole clique would jump in to attack me, loudly disrupting the rest of the class.

It was a difficult and painful struggle, but slowly, over the year, we all learned something. The quieter students, much more aware of the needs of the whole, felt threatened by this powerful clique and spent most of the year in silence, gradually learning to speak up and take care of themselves. The girls in the power clique slowly gained compassion and awareness. I continued to struggle with wanting to look good, wanting to control, and a shortcoming that kept coming up—wanting to be liked.

I see I have to let go of the desire to be liked by my students in order to contribute fully to them. I see that confronting them about their commitments and broken agreements is necessary, but it is very difficult to remember it, do it, and keep doing it in the face of their abusiveness. Finally, I started to turn it over to my own inner voice. I tried to stay present, be with whatever circumstances the moment would bring, and trust that everything is perfect just the way it is, no matter how it looks. Then, I would react differently to each situation. There are no rules, just opportunities to practice being with uncertainty.

The pain was almost unbearable at times. But it was the pain of my doubt—that maybe the consensus classroom doesn't work—that was most difficult. It does work, because no matter what each of us brings in, we all come out with just the learning we need. This is learning that cannot be measured, documented, or proved; it can just be known.

ow We Know It Works

The growth of the human mind is still high adventure, in many ways the highest adventure on earth.—Norman Cousins

The case for the multiage, continuous progress classrooms needs ways to prove that students progress in a manner similar to the more traditional classrooms. Without valid assessment tools that work across the grade levels, prudent educators are reluctant to embrace the idea. Fortunately, authentic assessment models do just that. Three articles in particular are collected in this final section that target assessing the multiage classroom. While these evaluation tools are appropriate for assessing students in all classrooms, they are especially useful for the mixed-aged groupings and the unique concerns that accompany nongradedness.

Goodman's essay on "Kidwatching" provides ideas for observing children interacting within the rich learning environment of the whole language classroom. Through specific examples, the author analyzes the children's development and shows how these examples provide fertile ground for teacher insight. In particular, the "unexpected response" is discussed, as well as ideas about where to start and what to do.

A second essay highlights the use of portfolios as valuable assessment tools for the mixed-age classroom. In this piece, Burke defines portfolios, provides rationale, and discusses how portfolios are best utilized. Practical ideas are listed clearly and concisely in procedural way for easy implementation. In addition, grading options are discussed, as well as methods for conducting the portfolio conference.

Jeroski and Brownlie conclude this section with a practical article entitled, "How Do We Know We're Getting Better?" Filled with examples of student work, the authors explore evaluation from the perspective of how students make choices and connections as well as how to determine if the student's depth of understanding is powerful, competent, partial or undeveloped. The authors conclude with a look at assessing thoughtful interactions and the use of meaningful tasks in evaluation.

Kidwatching: Observing Children in the Classroom

by Yetta M. Goodman

T hree first graders were grouped around the flotation bowl. They were trying to discover what things could float and why. Elana put a wadded piece of foil in the bowl. Just as it sank to the bottom, Mr. Borton walked up and observed the scene. He noticed a wet, fair-sized aluminum boat next to the bowl.

He addressed the group, "What did you just learn?"

Elana responded quickly, "Big things float and small things sink."

Robin reacted, "Uh, uh. I don't think that's always true."

"What might you do to prove the hypothesis Elana just made?" said Borton.

"Well," said Lynn, "Maybe we could make a small boat and a big ball and try those things to see what will happen." As the children got involved in the new tasks they set for themselves, Borton walked on to another group.

> Good teachers, like Mr. Borton, have always been kid-watchers.

Good teachers, like Mr. Borton, have always been kid-watchers. The concept of kid-watching is not new. It grows out of the child study movement that reached a peak in the 1930s providing a great deal of knowledge about human growth and development. Teachers can translate child study into its most universal form: learning about children by watching how they learn. The term kid-watching has caught on among those who believe that children learn language best in an environment rich

Excerpted from *Observing the Language Learner*, Angela Jaggar and M. Trika Smith-Burke (International Reading Association, 1985) p. 9–17. Reprinted with permission.

with opportunities to explore interesting objects and ideas. Through observing the reading, writing, speaking, and listening of friendly, interactive peers, interested, kidwatching teachers can understand and support child language development.

Evaluation of the progress of conceptual and language development for individual children cannot be provided in any useful sense by formalized pencil and paper tests. Evaluation provides the most significant information if it occurs continuously and simultaneously with the experiences in which the learning is taking place. Borton knows a lot about how children conceptualize, develop new insights into the physical nature of the world, and what kinds of language they use and have developed during the activity in which they were involved.

Even in the home, parents are aware of how much their children have grown, whether they have become better ball players or how much more considerate they have become toward other family members. Parents know this by their constant attention to and involvement with size of clothes, the faster and harder return of a pitched ball, or some deed a child does for a parent or sibling. Scales and yardsticks may provide some statistical data for parents to use to verify their observational knowledge, but it is never a lone measure on which they rely.

Unfortunately, especially in recent years, scores on tests have been viewed as more objective than the judgment of a professional observer since test results are often presented under an aura of statistical "significance" which for many people has an unquestionable mystique.

Formal tests, standardized or criterion referenced, provide statistical measures of the product of learning but only as supplementary evidence for professional judgments about the growth of children. If teachers rely on formalized tests they come to conclusions about children's growth based on data from a single source. Tests do provide evidence of how children grow in their ability to handle test situations but not in their ability to handle settings where important language learnings occur. Studies of the role that context plays in how children learn have made it clear that children respond differently in different situations. Teachers who observe the development of language and knowledge in children in different settings become aware of important milestones in children's development that tests cannot reveal.

Kidwatching, the focus of this [chapter], is used as a slogan to reinstate and legitimize the significance of professional observation in the classroom. Those who support such child study understand that the evaluation of pupils' growth and curriculum development are integrally related. The energies of teachers and other curriculum planners must go into building a powerful learning environment. The key question in evaluation is not, "Can the child perform the specific tasks that have been taught?" Rather, the question is, "Can the child adjust language used in other situations to meet the demands of new settings?" The teacher must be aware that children learn all the time. The best way to gain insight into language learning is to observe children using language to explore all kinds of concepts in art, social studies, math, science, or physical education.

> **The teacher must be aware that children learn all the time.**

Teachers screen their observations through their philosophy, their knowledge base, and their assumptions whenever they are involved in kidwatching. Following are some of the basic premises which underlie kidwatching notions:

1. Current knowledge about child language and conceptual development must be a part of continuous education for teachers. Such knowledge guides observations. Not only does it help teachers know what to look for as signs of growth and development but it also helps teachers become consciously aware of their knowledge, their biases, and their philosophical orientation.

2. Language and concepts grow and develop depending on the settings in which they occur, the experiences that children have in those settings, and the interaction of the people in those settings. The richer and more varied these settings and interactions, the richer the child's language and concepts will be.

3. Knowledgeable teachers ready to assume responsibility for observation and evaluation of children play a very significant role in enriching the child's development of language and concepts.

CURRENT KNOWLEDGE ABOUT LANGUAGE

During the second half of this century a knowledge explosion has occurred in the study of language or linguistics. Much of this knowledge is contrary to the ideas about language which have been taught in the past under the labels of phonics, spelling, vocabulary, and grammar. In addition, there have been enormous gains in understandings about how children learn language. When old beliefs are being questioned and new knowledge is not fully understood, a great deal of controversy is often generated. This is especially true of those who have to apply the knowledge, as teachers do in classroom situations. Since much of the new information that must be considered by kidwatchers will be presented in the following chapters, only a few aspects of language variation and the role of error in language learning will be touched on here.

There are many issues concerning language differences in the areas of both dialect and second language learning which teachers must consider. Too many children have been hurt in the past because of lack of knowledge about language differences. Not only teachers but test makers and curriculum builders often produce materials that reflect myths and misunderstandings. The more knowledge teachers have about language variation, the better position they are in to evaluate materials and tests in order to use them wisely and appropriately. Attitudes such as "these children have no language" or "bilingualism confuses children" are still too prevalent. Kidwatching can help teachers be aware of how such statements are damaging to language growth, if they are armed with up-to-date knowledge. By observing the language of children in a wide variety of settings such as role playing, retelling of picture books, or playing games during recess or physical education, teachers gain many kinds of information that help to dispel myths about language and language learning.

For example, Sorita, age six, would use the following types of construction often in oral conversations with other children or during sharing sessions:

"Lots of my friends was at my house...."
"We was going to the store...."

However, during her narration of "The Three Billy Goats Gruff" which accompanied the acting out of the story by some of her classmates, her teachers heard, "There were three billy goats...." Sorita used this more formal construction throughout the narration.

Retelling a story, about a farmer and his son, a recent nine year old immigrant from Lebanon said, "They were working at to plant something."

Both examples provide insight into each child's language development. Sorita shows the ability to use the more formal "were" form in storytelling although she uses the colloquial form in the informal settings. She is aware of formal and informal language settings and that each permits different language.

The second child shows growing control over two kinds of complex English structures—the verb plus particle "working at" and the infinitive form "to plant," even though as this child combines the structures, they may sound a little unusual to a native English speaker's ear.

Errors in language and in conceptual development reflect much more than a mistake that can be eradicated with a red pencil or a verbal admonition. What an adult perceives as wrong may in actuality reflect development in the child. Errors, miscues, or misconceptions usually indicate ways in which a child is organizing the world at that moment. As children develop conceptually and linguistically, their errors shift from those that represent unsophisticated conclusions to ones that show greater sophistication. The previous examples are evidence of this kind of growth. Sometimes teachers expect certain responses or "correct answers" because of a school based cultural view of the world. The child's unexpected responses, if observed with understanding, may broaden a teacher's conceptualization about the child's world. "Errors" also indicate interpretations which may in no way be wrong but simply show that the child has used inferences about reading or listening which were unexpected.

For example, a kindergarten teacher gave her class a short talk about what was wrong with wasting milk prior to morning snack time. Tomasa was observed taking a small sip of milk. She

> What an adult perceives as wrong may in actuality reflect development in the child.

then carefully closed the milk carton, wiped her place with her paper towel, and slowly placed the carton of milk in the waste basket, holding it tight until it reached the bottom.

"Didn't we just talk about not wasting milk?" Miss Dasson asked.

"I ain't waste my milk," Tomasa responded. "I keeped everything real clean!"

Miss Dasson now knows that "waste" has an alternate meaning in the language of Tomasa's community—"to spill." She and Tomasa can now share each other's meanings.

The kidwatcher who understands the role of unexpected responses will use children's errors and miscues to chart their growth and development and to understand the personal and cultural history of the child. There are no tests available which can provide this kind of data to the professional educator. These insights can emerge only from kidwatching based on a sound knowledge of language and language learning.

Individual teachers may not be in a position to keep current about the dynamic information so vital to understanding language learning. However, courses of study or programs can be organized through setting up teacher support groups, working cooperatively with teacher educators at local universities and colleges or with inservice personnel at the district level, and holding discussion groups. Although courses in linguistics, the science of language, many in themselves be helpful, it may be more useful if teachers encourage and participate in the development of programs which have an applied orientation for the classroom.

VARIATIONS OF SETTING, FUNCTION, AND MATERIAL
Thoughtful observation of children takes place in a rich, innovative curriculum in the hands of a knowledgeable teacher who demands and accepts responsibility for curriculum decision making. With such teachers, children are involved in exciting educational experiences and make the greatest growth in language learning and conceptual development.

Curriculum becomes sterilized when it is based on pupils' results on standardized tests or progress on "criterion referenced" behavioral checksheets. In order to achieve appropriate gains, curriculum experiences must narrow to those safely entombed in the test itself. Curriculum becomes repetitive practice with the same kind of "skills" on workbooks and worksheets as in the test. The only individualization is how much practice each pupil must endure.

Where kidwatching is an integral part of the curriculum, the teacher's focus is on providing rich learning experiences for children. There is an awareness of the dynamic relationship among the teacher, the children, and the experiences. Evaluation is ongoing. Although teachers should certainly be expected to document and discuss the growth of their children, the most important role of the teacher is involving children in learning through the richness of the curriculum. Only when children have a variety of materials available to read and many good personal reasons to want to learn about new ideas and concepts will they read various genre, write for different purposes, and grow in their ability to use written language effectively.

> Where kidwatching is an integral part of the curriculum, the teacher's focus is on providing rich learning experiences for children.

As functions and purposes for learning new concepts change, so will the settings, the language, and the materials needed for the learnings change. These broadened experiences enrich language learning for children and provide many opportunities for kidwatching to occur. Children must go to the library to solve certain problems, to the principal's office to solve others. They interview some people orally, read about others, or write letters as it serves the purposes of their explorations. Language learning reaches out to meet new challenges and teachers can evaluate the flexibility with which children can expand language use.

For example, keeping copies of children's letters written to different people over the course of a few months provides evidence about: 1) the appropriateness of the language of the letters, depending on their purposes; 2) the degree to which children change the language and style of the letters, depending on their audience; 3) the increase of conventionally spelled words over time; 4) changes in the complexity of grammatical structures; and 5) concern for legibility.

TEACHER'S ROLE IS SIGNIFICANT

Concepts from three scholars in different fields of child study provide a jumping off place from which to explore the significance of the teacher's role. Jerome Bruner talks about "scaffolding"; M.A.K. Halliday, about "tracking"; and L.S. Vygotsky, about the "zone of proximal development." Each of these concepts is used to express the significance of communicative interactions between adults and children which are basic to the expansion of language and the extension of learning in children. If parents play as significant a role a child's language development as these scholars suggest, it seems logical that a teacher with understandings about how children learn language might capitalize on their ideas and be even more effective than parents in supporting child language growth and extending it once the child comes to school.

Focusing on mother/child interaction, Bruner (1978) defines scaffolding by quoting Roger Brown:

> A study of detailed mother/child interaction…shows that successful communication on one level is always the launching platform for attempts at communication on a more adult level. (p. 251)

Bruner continues:

> The mother systematically changes her BT(Baby Talk) in order to "raise the ante" or alter the conditions she imposes on the child's speech in different settings. (p. 251)

According to Bruner (1978), the adult always takes the child's ideas seriously, thinking through what the child is trying to communicate, allowing the child to move ahead when capable of doing so, and supporting the child only when the child seems to need help.

> Once the child has made a step forward, she (the mother) will not let him slide back. She assures that he go on with the next construction to develop a next platform for his next launch. (p. 254).

Halliday (1982) uses a similar notion about language learning in children which he calls tracking. From his extensive study about language development, Halliday concludes that the adults and older siblings who live with the child "share in the language-creating process along with the child" (p.10). He suggests that teachers take on a similar role when the child comes to school, helping children find new ways to say or write things as children find new reasons to express themselves or to understand.

> Observation, evaluation, and curriculum planning go hand-in-hand.

Vygotsky (1962) who adds additional perspectives on the significance of child/adult interaction, believes that educators can make use of cooperation between adult and student and "lead the child to what he could not yet do" (p.104) by himself.

Vygotsky defines the "discrepancy between a child's actual mental age and the level he reaches in solving problems with assistance" (p.103) as the child's zone of proximal development.

> With assistance every child can do more than he can by himself…What the child can do in cooperation today, he can do alone tomorrow. Therefore, the only good kind of instruction is that which marches ahead of development and leads it, it must be aimed not so much at the ripe as at the ripening functions. (p. 103-104).

Although there may be some theoretical differences among these scholars, there is little disagreement about the significance of the role of the teacher or other adults involved in children's growth. Teachers who continually observe children using knowledge about language and cognition can ask the appropriate question, or pose a specific problem, or place an object in front of children so that learning is extended. As they observe, they also gain information for planning new experiences or instructional activities, leading the child toward new explorations. Observation, evaluation, and curriculum planning go hand-in-hand.

Teachers can develop a variety of ways to keep records of these developments for reporting to parents, to remind themselves of children's growth over the year, to involve students in self-evaluation, and to leave records for continued school use. However, the records of kidwatchers are not simply statistics used to compare children nor to have them compete with one another. Whether they are anecdotal records of children's inter-actions; selected writing samples of students' letters, logs, and stories; or tapes of children's reading or oral reporting, their purpose is to provide profiles of the children's language growth in different settings, with different materials, and through different experiences.

WHERE TO START? WHAT TO DO?

My own observations of outstanding kidwatching teachers are reflected in the following suggestions:

1. *When a child achieves success in some communicative setting (including reading and writing), the teacher may find a number of ways to extend this to a new and different setting.* For example, a child who is responding orally to a patterned language book such as "I Know an Old Woman Who Swallowed a Fly" can be encouraged to write a book either alone, with the teacher, or a peer entitled "Johnny Swallowed a Bumblebee." This would extend the holistically remembered oral reading of a book to writing a book to share with others using similar language structures but personalizing characters and experiences in writing. But don't expect the new use of communication to look as successful as the one previously achieved. When a child tries something new it is bound to seem less sophisticated at first than something the child does which is familiar.

2. *When children are involved in exploratory activities, the teacher might raise questions such as "I wonder why this is so?" or "What do you think is happening here?"* The questions may help children reflect on their own thinking and see contradictions in their hypotheses.

3. *When children are observed to be troubled with an experience, the teacher can move in and talk about the situation with them and lead them to what they cannot yet do by themselves* (Vygotsky, 1962). It is at a moment of frustration that a kidwatching teacher can help children resolve conflictive situations à la Piaget (1977) and move on to expand their language and conceptualization.

4. *Teachers need to trust in children's learning and in their own ability to learn along with their children.* Language learning involves risk taking. When teachers believe in their own profes-

sional judgment and respect the children's ability, success occurs as part of the curricular experiences. With such a sense of security teachers can become kidwatchers and with the children build a community which contains many launching pads from which the children and the teacher can reach the next level of language learning together.

What Is a Portfolio?

by Kay Burke

Aportfolio is a collection of a student's work that connects separate items to form a clearer, more complete picture of the student as a lifelong learner. Portfolios can contain a repertoire of assessments such as observation checklists, logs, journals, videos, cassettes, pictures, projects, and performances. These different types of assessments allow students to display every aspect of their capabilities. A portfolio contains several separate pieces that may not mean much by themselves, but when compiled together, they produce a more accurate and holistic portrait of the student. "A portfolio is more than a 'folder' of student work; it is a deliberate, specific collection of accomplishments" (Hamm & Adams, 1991, p. 20).

Portfolios come in the form of file folders, hanging folders, notebooks, boxes, or video disks. They can include the work of one student or a group of students. They can cover one subject area or all the subject areas. They can be sent home at the end of the year or they can be stored in the school and passed on from year to year. They can include anecdotal records, whole class profiles, parent surveys, formal test results, narrative report cards, or any number of items selected by both the teacher and the student.

Elementary teachers can include all the subject areas in one portfolio. Middle school teachers could have students keep an integrated portfolio of the different subjects they take in their teams, and high school teachers can have students keep quarterly, semester, or yearly portfolios that may eventually become employment portfolios when the students graduate.

> "A portfolio is more than a 'folder' of student work; it is a deliberate, specific collection of accomplishments."

Excerpted from *The Mindful School: How to Assess Thoughtful Outcomes* (Palatine, IL: IRI/Skylight, 1993) p. 44–49. Reprinted with permission.

Some school systems are planning to use portfolios to monitor student growth from kindergarten to senior year. Often students leaving one grade share their portfolios with students coming into the grade so the new students know what to expect. Other systems allow students to keep their portfolios to monitor their own development over the years and to help them evaluate their own progress. Some portfolios are graded on the basis of predetermined criteria; others are used to help students reflect on their own progress and set goals for the future.

WHY SHOULD WE USE PORTFOLIOS?

Wolf (1989), Vavrus (1990), Paulson et al. (1991), Lazear (1991), and many others recommend using portfolios because they can be used as:

- Tools for discussion with peers, teachers, and parents
- Opportunities for students to demonstrate their skills and understanding
- Opportunities for students to reflect on their work
- Chances to set future goals
- Documentation of students' development and growth in ability, attitudes, and expression
- Demonstrations of different learning styles, multiple intelligences, cultural diversity
- Chances for students to make critical choices about what they select for their portfolio
- Opportunities for students to trace the development of their learning
- Opportunities for students to make connections between prior knowledge and new learning

Hansen (1992) advocates using self-created literacy portfolios where students include what they are like *outside* the classroom. Students can include pictures of relatives, awards, or ribbons they have won in athletic events, or lists of books or magazines about rock stars, sports, hobbies, or anything that interests them. The key to the portfolio is the discussion the items generate. Every adult and student in a literacy portfolios project creates a literacy portfolio. "Whether or not we know ourselves better than anyone else does, our portfolios give us the opportunity to get to know ourselves better" (Hansen, 1992, p. 66).

Krogness (1991) suggests that students list their goals at the beginning of each year. The goal setting allows them to learn what they value and address their concerns and interests by doing authentic work.

HOW SHOULD WE USE PORTFOLIOS?

Portfolios can reveal a great deal about each student. They allow teachers and students to understand the educational process at the level of the individual learner. "Portfolios allow students to assume ownership in ways that few other instructional approaches allow. Portfolio assessment requires students to collect and reflect on examples of their work.... If carefully assembled, portfolios become an intersection of instruction and assessment: they are not just instruction or just assessment but, rather, both. Together, instruction and assessment give more than either gives separately" (Paulson, Paulson, and Meyer, 1991, p. 61).

Teachers need to determine many things before beginning a portfolio program. Portfolio planning needs to be done before the first portfolio assignment is given. Teachers need to know the answers to the following questions before they begin a portfolio.

QUESTIONS TO ASK BEFORE BEGINNING A PORTFOLIO SYSTEM

1. What are the purposes of using a portfolio?
2. How should the pieces in the portfolio be selected?
3. What specific pieces should be included?
4. What are the evaluation options?
5. How should the portfolio be organized?
6. What are the options for conducting portfolio conferences?

The following checklists help individual teachers or groups of teachers decide how they can use portfolios to meet the needs of their students.

A. **How will the portfolio be used?**
  1. Is the entire portfolio going to move with the student from grade to grade, school to school?
  2. Will a few pieces be saved from each year as the portfolio is passed from grade to grade?
  3. Will it be sent home to the parents at the end of each year?
  4. Is it going to contain work from only one class (English, history), or from all the subject areas?
  5. Is it going to be used as a schoolwide or districtwide accountability piece to compare students with other students using pre-established criteria?
  6. Is it going to be used as a reflective piece so that students can look back at their work and see their own growth and development?
  7. Will it be used for self-evaluation by the student?
  8. Is it going to be used for parent conferences?
  9. Have the pieces in the portfolio been graded prior to handing in the finished portfolio? (Therefore, there is no grade on the portfolio.)
  10. Is it going to be assessed as part of the final grade?

B. **How should the pieces in the portfolio be selected?**
  1. Should some works that are "still in progress" be included?
  2. Should only finished products be contained in the portfolio?
  3. Should students select only their "best" work?
  4. Should the students select all the pieces to be included in the portfolio?
  5. Should the teacher select all the pieces to be included in the portfolio?
  6. Should the teachers and the students share in the selection process of the portfolio's content?
  7. Should teacher comments about the students' work be included?
  8. Should peer comments about the portfolio be included?

C. **What specific pieces should be included in the portfolio?**
  1. Homework
  2. Teacher-made quizzes and tests
  3. Peer editing assignments

4. Group work (artifacts or pictures)
5. Learning logs
6. Problem-solving logs
7. Reflective journals
8. Community projects
9. Written work
10. Rough drafts of written work to show process
11. Cassettes of speeches, readings, singing, questioning techniques
12. Graphic organizers
13. Questions for a conference
14. Questionnaires about attitudes and opinions
15. Interviews with other students
16. Observation checklists (self or group)
17. Metacognitive activities
18. Self-assessments
19. Letter to teacher or parents about contents of portfolio
20. Statement of future goals
21. Free pick (no criteria given)
22. Pictures of performances such as speeches, plays, debates, historical re-enactments
23. Pictures of individual projects or group projects that are too big to include
24. A registry or log where students date and discuss when and why they log in an entry and when they take out an entry
25. Computer programs
26. Lab experiments
27. Samples of artwork (or pictures)
28. Videos of performances

D. **What are the evaluation options?**
1. Students' work is assessed throughout the course. Therefore, the final portfolio is **not graded**; it is just a tool to allow students and parents to see growth and development over time.
2. **One grade** is given to the entire portfolio on the basis of the body of work included. The grade is based on criteria that have been predetermined by both the students and the teacher.

3. **Each piece** of work in the portfolio is **graded separately** on the basis of predetermined criteria for each assignment.

4. **No grade** is given on the final portfolio, but a few pieces from each subject area are collected in one integrated portfolio to represent the body of work of a student for a year. The portfolio is sent home to the parents or passed on to the next year's teacher.

5. **Several pieces** from the portfolio are **passed on to the next teacher** the next year. Each year some pieces will be removed and others will be added in order to compile a body of work for a graduating senior.

6. The **senior portfolio** is used in the interview process for a job or college.

E. **How can the portfolio be organized?**

1. **Creative cover** that reflects the personality or interests of the student

2. **Table of contents** that includes the items and page numbers of the pieces of work contained in the portfolio

3. The **contents** of the portfolio organized according to the table of contents

4. A **written comment** about each item in the portfolio telling why the item was selected and how the student feels about it

5. A **self-assessment** of the portfolio by the student

6. A list of **future goals** based on the students' needs, interests, and self-assessment of the portfolio

7. A **letter** from the teacher or parents to the student including comments, feedback, and encouragement

F. **What are the options for conducting portfolio conferences?**

1. **Student-Teacher:** The student can discuss the portfolio with the teacher.

2. **Student-Student:** Each student can share the contents of his or her portfolio with peers.

3. **Student-Cooperative Group Members:** Each member of the cooperative group can share his or her portfolio with group members.

4. **Cross-Age:** Students in one grade can share their port-

folios with students in another grade.

5. **Student-Parent:** Students can conduct their own portfolio conference at home or at official school conferences.

6. **Student-Parent-Teacher:** The participants talk about portfolios at school and set up video stations to show performances and projects.

7. **Student-Parent Conference at Home:** Students take the portfolio home to show and explain to parents. A question guide helps parents ask thoughtful questions.

8. **Significant Other:** Student invites a friend, teacher, brother, sister, or parent to school for a portfolio conference during school hours or after school.

9. **Portfolio Exhibitions:** Students display portfolios at an exhibition and explain their work to visitors.

10. **Pen Pal:** Students mail a few items from portfolios to pen pals and solicit comments or suggestions.

CONCLUSION

The portfolio assessment system cannot succeed without the teacher's forethought and planning. The teacher must begin by answering essential questions about the purpose, organization, and evaluation of the portfolio. However, the ultimate responsibility belongs to the students to assume ownership of and take pride in their accomplishments. By working with the teacher to select and collect pieces to include in the portfolio, the students continually connect their prior knowledge with new learning. Through this active reflection, the portfolio becomes a true tool for lifelong learning.

How Do We Know We're Getting Better?

by Sharon Jeroski and Faye Brownlie

The minute we begin to articulate our feelings, ideas, and judgments about a piece of literature, it begins to take another shape. We see things we had not seen before, and we begin to forget those things that do not relate to the account we are giving of the story. This is true whether we are simply retelling the story to friend, asking a question of a trusted colleague, expressing our opinions to a stranger on the street, or pausing a moment to talk silently to ourselves about what we have just read.—(Nelms, 1988, p. 7)

Teachers today are struggling to reconcile their beliefs about how students develop as thoughtful, responsive readers with their need to offer clear evidence that students are becoming "better" readers. It seems clear that traditional indicators such as standardized test scores, percent correct, or rank-in-class do not offer the kinds of information teachers find helpful in supporting students who are actively constructing meaning as they read. What features might characterize assessment of authentic achievement in reading real accomplishments of active, responsive readers?

- The student makes critical choices about such features as materials, use of time, and representation of response.
- The student makes connections with previous knowledge and experience in shaping a response.
- The student personalizes the reading experience and shows some depth of understanding.

Excerpted from *If Minds Matter: A Foreword to the Future*, vol. 2 (Palatine, IL: IRI/Skylight, 1992) p. 321–336. Reprinted with permission.

- The student's response reflects or stimulates thoughtful interactions about the reading experience.
- The text and the response task are meaningful to the student.

MAKING CRITICAL CHOICES

Active readers are continually making choices—choices about what they will read, when they will read, and how they will read. They also make choices about what they will do with their reading—how they will respond and represent their ideas, and whether or not they will seek an audience.

In working with young readers, we very quickly discovered that assessing and evaluating their development was much easier when we encouraged them to make their own choices. Rather than offering carefully structured reading assignments, we began inviting the students to use their feelings, ideas, and images to demonstrate their understanding of a reading. Freed from our expectations, the children responded in wonderful and diverse ways. In Louise Zappitello's primary classroom, children aged six to nine have frequent opportunities to make choices about their reading and their representations.

Miya

Miya is an eight-year-old author and illustrator who is strongly drawn to the imagery of poetry (See Figure 1). Miya explained, "I thought it would be fun to show you what the bug was thinking. I put myself into the bug's mind and I got a really strong picture of the kind of town it might like." Miya's illustration offers a delightful personal perspective with "Les Miserables" playing at the local Bug Mall. Miya's "bug"—like Miya herself—is enjoying the images it has created.

Miya is also the principal illustrator of the collaborative novel she is working on. "I write the words and draw the pictures; they [her partners] color them," she explains. The novel features three beautiful, rich, and independent young women who move from one fortunate adventure to another. It is carefully written and exquisitely illustrated.

Stina

In the same classroom, Stina (who is collaborating on a mystery novel) chose to read and respond to a poem about a dog "thin

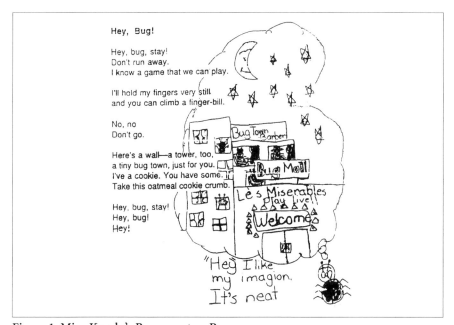

Figure 1 Miya Kondo's Response to a Poem
From *Reading and Responding* by Jeroski, S., Brownlie, F., & Kaser, L. Copyright 1991. Used by permission of Nelson, Canada, a division of Thomson Canada Limited.

as a rail" whose fleas hop from the bottom to the top whenever he waves his tail. Stina wrote:

> I wonder why he only hase flees on his tail but if he hase fles on his tail why whene he waves his tail they don't go all over his body. If he is as thin as a rail he must not be a healthy dog. where do the fleas that are on the top go whene he waves his tail.

Stina has a dog and she is intrigued by some of the detail in the poem. In conversation she explained that her dog sometimes had fleas, but he was much healthier than the dog in the poem. Stina is characteristically curious—she poses a number of questions that demonstrate her connections to what she already knows about dogs: Why does he only have fleas on his tail? Why when he waves his tail don't they go all over his body? As an author, Stina is currently much more interested in exploring and playing with language and ideas than with illustrations and images. We see these choices extending to her novel, which she and her partner, Tim, have been working on intermittently for several weeks.

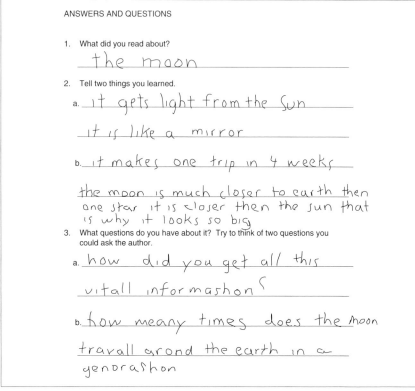

ANSWERS AND QUESTIONS

1. What did you read about?

the moon

2. Tell two things you learned.

a. it gets light from the Sun

it is like a mirror

b. it makes one trip in 4 weeks

the moon is much closer to earth then one star it is closer then the sun that is why it looks so big

3. What questions do you have about it? Try to think of two questions you could ask the author.

a. how did you get all this vitall informashon

b. how meany times does the moon travall arond the earth in a genorashon

Figure 2 Stina's Answers and Questions

Stina and Tim are obviously enjoying their collaboration, although they explain that they sometimes get tired of their book and stop writing it for a week or two. It features a complex Halloween/mystery plot and they explain that they usually get their ideas by talking together, "but sometimes when we're writing we really don't know what's going to happen." Although they are keen to find a new audience for their novel, they have obviously had so much fun writing it that sharing it is almost anticlimactic.

Stina's enthusiasm for language and learning is also apparent when she selects **answers and questions** as a way of demonstrating her understanding of a selection about the moon (See Figure 2). (Children were offered four choices: illustrating; writing a note to someone at home; writing about the new information they learned; or answers and questions).

Although the assignment asks for two pieces of information, Stina includes as much as possible. Her questions are delightful—clearly the questions of a developing author who loves language. She wants to find out where the author got all this vital information and how many times the moon travels around the earth in a generation.

The wide range of representations of thinking reflects the opportunities present in the classroom. These children recognize their ability to both choose from among a repertoire and to apply their choices in a variety of contexts. All of the children were able to choose both reading material and ways of responding and representing without teacher support. This was definitely a skill that had been practiced. Louise frequently meets with her class to talk about their shared reading, the independently chosen books they are reading, and the choices they make when they represent their ideas. Discussion focuses around questions such as:

Choosing Books:

- How did you pick that book? Was it a good choice for you?

- Who do you know that might like this book? Why do you think they would like it?

- Do you ever give other people advice about books and stories they might like? Who do you give advice to? Do you think your advice helps them?

- Who tells you about good books to read? How do their ideas help you?

- What books have surprised you—books that you thought you might not like that turned out to be interesting? Books that you thought you would like but found out you didn't?

- What do you do when you find you have made a mistake in choosing a book?

- What do you usually do when you finish reading a book? (Do you tell other students about it? Write about it? Read it again?)

Choosing Responses:

- What are some of the ways you like to represent your ideas?

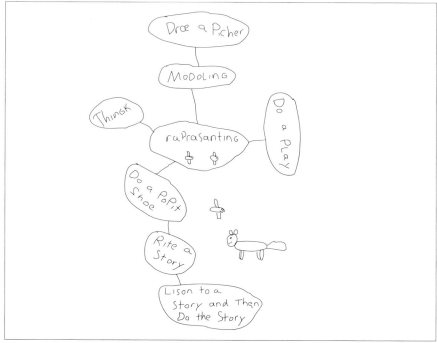

Figure 3 Student's Diagram of Representations

- What are some of the ways you like other people to represent their ideas when they are sharing with you?

- How do you like to represent your ideas when you are working with a partner? With a group? With an older or a younger buddy? Outside of school?

- What kinds of representations do other people ask you to help them with?

- What kinds of representations do you avoid? What kinds would you like to be better at?

- What kinds of responses or representations does your teacher usually like best?

  (Adapted from *Thinking in the Classroom*, Ministry of Education, 1991.)

The teachers and students we work with value and monitor the choices they make through their oral and written reflections in conferences, learning and thinking logs, portfolios, and classroom sign-up sheets where they indicate the genres, books, stories, and forms they are currently exploring (See Figure 3).

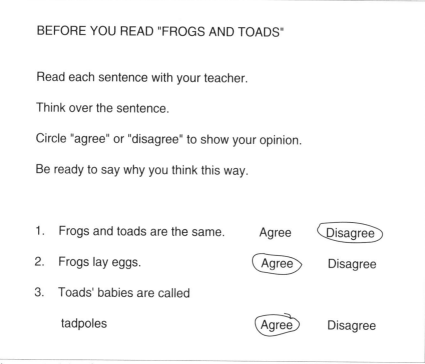

Figure 4 Activity Sheet to Encourage Connection Making

MAKING CONNECTIONS

Connecting—between the known and the unknown, with others, with personal experience, and with the world—is fundamental to assessing growth in learning. Children can be encouraged to connect their prior experiences with reading by activities such as in Figure 4.

The importance of the connections is made explicit by the teacher's question: "Does the information agree with your ideas?" Jenna, a seven-year-old in Lynn Hoeteker's class, clearly indicates that while reading, she has held her prior knowledge in mind and looked for substantiating evidence (See Figure 5).

But there is more to reading then just connecting with what you already know. Readers also can learn new things and wonder about others. Jenna's thinking is extended by her teacher's prompts (See Figure 6).

These prompts provide connections to the world outside the classroom—now Jenna is searching for new connections.

Read "Frogs and Toads." Does the information agree with

your ideas?

1 agree

2 Yes because it showed an egg
and there was some informashon
on the egg

3 the auther agreed because
he said that the egg turns
in to a tadpole

Figure 5 Jenna's Responsible to Reading "Frogs and Toads"

ANSWERS AND QUESTIONS

1. What did you read about?

frogs and todes

2. Tell two things you learned.

a. that frogs don't only eat flys
and mosquitoes

b. frogs lay jelly eggs

3. What questions do you have about it? Try to think of two questions you
could ask the author.

a. why do frog and todes
leap high

b. what do tadpoles look like
when they just com out of an egg

Figure 6 Jenna's Answers and Questions

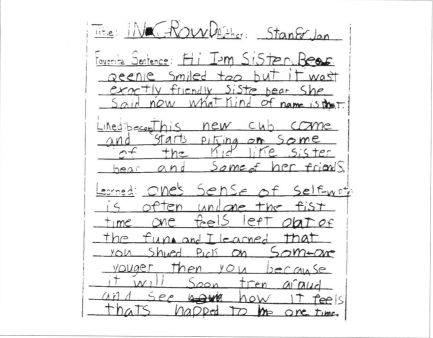

Figure 7 Michael's Response to a Reading

In Linda Kaser's classroom, students examine their independent reading from three perspectives: a favorite sentence, what they liked, and what they learned. Michael was able to respond from all three perspectives (See Figure 7).

Michael's "learned" reflection connects the experience of the character not only to a global lesson (not to pick on someone younger than you) but also to his personal world (that's what happened to me one time). Michael chose a book that was meaningful to him: Linda offered a task that supported him in making sense of his reading. In turn, he provided her with clear, valid information about his development as a reader.

Another way to examine the connections with content or expanding bodies of knowlege is through learning log prompts such as "I used to think…but now…" Reflections such as this help students recognize their need to make connections and adapt existing schema as new learning reconnects and reshapes information. For example, after studying a unit on trees, two eight-year-olds in Laura Smith's library reflected:

> I used to not know that trees had patterns but now I know that they do. I can tell the difference of the trees because of the patterns. I used to think trees were not useful, but now I know they give us paper and oxygen.

> I used to think all the trees had…leaves. But now I know not all trees have leaves—they have needles. I used to think trees weren't useful. But now I know they breathe carbon dioxide.

Collaborative Connections

The power of collaborative learning is emphasized by prompting students to reflect on their connections with others in the class. Notice how this six-year-old's entry informs us as to what students know about learning—the value of expertise, the willingness of people to share their ideas, and the strengths of individuals within groups.

> Jay has tote me. I think more than 1 hanjrid things abuot ANTS. (Jay has taught me. I think more than 100 things about ants.)

Teachers' questions help students to make connections in their reading and thinking.

- What did we do today that helped us to become better learners? How did it help?
- How can we use what we learned?
- What did you notice about your thinking in this class today?
- How can you use the reading and thinking strategies we worked on today in your other classes? Outside of school? At work?
- Who helped you today? Whom did you help?
- What did you like about your reading today? What was challenging in your reading today?
- What was something you learned from reading that surprised you?
- What are questions which you are still curious about and would like to find some answers to?
- What are new questions you thought of after talking to your group?

DEPTH OF UNDERSTANDING

What kinds of indicators are appropriate for describing the depth and personalization of students' responses to their reading? We developed the following criteria and categories from the responses of students from ages eight through seventeen (Jeroski, Brownlie, & Kaser, 1990). The scales can be adapted to any age: for example, we have found it more helpful with younger children (ages four to seven) to describe three levels of responses (powerful, developing, and supported) rather than the four listed below (Jeroski, Brownlie, & Kaser, 1990).

The scoring guide and comments offer models for teachers and students to use in developing criteria in their own classrooms. The samples reprinted in Figures 8, 9, and 10 are from sixth grade students who had responded to a poem entitled "The Wild Wolves of Winter."

Powerful

The response is personalized and thoughtful. The student integrates previous experience and includes specific references to the text. The ideas expressed go beyond the text, describe the comparisons or metaphors, and indicate a relatively deep or sophisticated understanding of the selection.

Competent

The response is consistent and logical and features some integration of previous experience and includes text references. The student may focus on one aspect of the poem, not describe the metaphor, or deal with the idea on a surface level.

Partial

Some inconsistencies are apparent, suggesting a partial or incomplete understanding of the poem. Typically, the student makes less frequent use of images, emotions, and specific text references.

Undeveloped

The response is inconsistent or illogical. The student may offer broad general statements without explanation. If any text references are included, they may be inappropriate or illogical.

SAMPLE POWERFUL RESPONSE: John has captured the events of the blizzard and the howling wind in his drawings. The stark comparisons between the wolves' power and the people's helplessness are portrayed.

Figure 8　Student Response to the "Wolves of Winter"

From *Reading and Responding Grade 6* by Jeroski, S., Brownlie, F., & Kaser, L. Copyright 1990. Used by permission of Nelson Canada, a division of Thomson Canada Limited.

THOUGHTFUL INTERACTIONS

Student interviews are one way of finding out what students think about their developing competencies, what their personal evaluation of their growth is, and what support is needed to continue to enhance their language development.

Colin is a seven-year-old reader. He has practiced reading the age-old tale "The Turnip" and has now taped this reading.

SAMPLE PARTIAL RESPONSE: Lauren identified with the poet, the sleeplessness, and the fear, but she attributes this all to a pack of wolves. She has not recognized the wolves as representatives of a winter wind.

life for me is scary because packs of wolves keep on coming though my village. My life is also very sleepless because the wolves scrach at my door every night and keep me awake. I wish that the wolves will go back were they came from.

Lauren

Figure 9 Student Response to the "Wolves of Winter"
From *Reading and Responding Grade 6* by Jeroski, S., Brownlie, F., & Kaser, L. Copyright 1990. Used by permission of Nelson Canada, a division of Thomson Canada Limited.

He is interviewed by his teacher on his reading of the selection. His reading has been very expressive. Each time he came to the repeated line, "But the turnip wouldn't budge," the line became louder and more expressive. He made one miscue—"hungry" for "huge" but corrected himself after realizing that it was unlikely the turnip being pulled from the ground was "hungry."

Teacher: What did you think about your reading on the tape?

Colin: Quite good but for one word when I was practicing it. I felt a little better, then I made a couple of mistakes but I corrected them.

Teacher: Can you tell me about those mistakes?

SAMPLE COMPETENT RESPONSE: Jim understands the metaphor of the blizzard, but does not provide much detail in his description of it. He uses text information and personally responds to the fierce wind.

I think in the poem "The Wild Wolves of Winter" the wolves wher like a blizzard. The scratches at the door are like when the wind blows and you're all allone you Could almost think there was someone at the door. The poem is good

Jim

SAMPLE UNDEVELOPED RESPONSE: Lindsay attempts to interpret the wolf in the poem, but misses the intent and seriousness of the poet.

The Wild Woives of winter   Lindsay

I think this poem is about a person wearing a wolf skin jacket trying to stay intsead of outside in the cold.

Figure 10 Student Responses to the "Wolves of Winter"

From *Reading and Responding Grade 6* by Jeroski, S., Brownlie, F., & Kaser, L. Copyright 1990. Used by permission of Nelson Canada, a division of Thomson Canada Limited.

Colin: Hungry didn't make sense…a man pulling up a "hungry" turnip. So I asked my Mom and she said it was "huge," so I just remembered it. I practiced a couple of times on our way out to dinner and I just kept getting better and better at it. I guess it was quite great except leaving out the "huge" or "hungry."

Teacher: What would you like me to notice about your reading when I am listening to the tape?

Colin: My voice and stuff and how smoothly I was. How it is important in my voice that I put life into it. For example, "But the turnip wouldn't budge!" I make it like it's alive.

Colin's response clearly indicates what he values in his reading development. He prepares to read for an audience, recognizes the entertainment value of real reading, practices for improvement, reads for meaning, and checks with others when he needs support. His ability to talk about his reading with such clarity helps us continue to support his growing independence as a reader and a thinker.

Thoughtful interactions between students and teachers can also occur in print. A critical element in keeping the interaction thoughtful is asking real questions of a real audience with a real purpose.

The following two letters are samples from a second grade class after the Canadian Fitness Test. The teacher had been away for the testing day so the substitute teacher asked the children to write to Miss Kaser, describing their participation in the events.

Dear Miss Kaser,
I slept in this morning and I missed the Canada Fitness Test. I felt a little sad, but I didn't worry and if I was in it I would know that I would do very well on every one of them.
Love, Bonnie

Dear Miss Kaser,
I liked Canada Fitness because I felt I did better than last year. I mostly liked the shuttle run because you got to pick up bean bags and drop them. I mostly liked the 50 meter run because I liked being timed and running through the two cones. When I ran it was like running through two lion statues only with one colour and one eye as round as round can be. The thing I didn't like about Canada Fitness was me and my partner always had to line up last.
from Elsa

Both letters show the students' understanding of the effect of their actions on their performance and their positive performance image. Strong personal voices come through in their letters. They are obviously used to being carefully listened to and are attempting to write to Miss Kaser about what she would want to hear about them.

Julie Davis, a high school English teacher, asked her students to tell her in writing the kinds of questions they most liked to respond to. These are two responses:

> I like a question that is slightly cryptic and makes you think. Another question I like is one where there is no correct answer, you just have to let your ideas flow smoothly.

> Puzzles have always appealed to me for the simple reason that you know there must be an obvious answer, though it may be hidden.

> I hate questions that require a choice of yes or no, for I have learned that there is a compromise, a mutual area, between the absolutes.

> Many likes and dislikes of questions originate over the topic.
>
> > Deanna

Deanna's response indicates not only that she has carefully thought through her preferences, but that she has also experience with questions which invite reasoning.

> My favorite kind of question is one that takes as little time as possible to do. The reason is because I'm always busy and have better things to do than answer big silly useless, school, brainstorming problems. Although I like to tackle *practical problems* that can be done with ingenuity and skills.
>
> > Scott

These are real questions for a real world. Scott's perspective refocuses us on the number of questions which are asked in school by people who already know the answers to their questions.

Another combination is that of the unknown audience, the conversation with someone whom you may know less well. In Linda Hoffman's fourth grade class, the students were writing

'Dear Reader' letters to insert at the beginning of their thinking logs. The purpose of the letter was to guide the reader when he or she looked through the log. Of particular interest in these letters is the students' sense of pride in their accomplishments and their means of describing what they really value in their learning.

> Dear Reader,
> This is my Thinking Log. I put a lot of work into this so please don't look for spelling, coloring, etc. Some of the things I would especially like you to look at is the ocean garbage one because I think it is wrong to make a dump out of a gorgeous ocean and killing all the ducks and fish. And another thing I would like you to read is the front page of my book it is how I felt about learning at the beginning of the year and I still feel the same way about learning and even better!
>
> Yours truly, Radel

> Dear Reader,
> I want you to read my book and see if you can find out how my feelings were when I did my Brain, my Collage, my kindergartin and my feelings poem and if you would have the same feelings. The one that I felt best about was thinking inventory. I thought that was my best creative thing. I like it because it showed what I like to do, what my dream was and what I think will happen to me in the future and that's what I think is important. I also think my learning has changed when I have to give a straight answer my learning isn't that different but when I can give all my ideas about it I think it shows you where I've changed in my learning.
>
> Thanks, Dustin

These letters reflect not only the sense of writing for a real audience, but students who have learned from a series of thoughtful experiences and interactions with one another and their teacher throughout the year.

MEANINGFUL TASKS

The ultimate goal of most reading instruction is the development of thoughtful, independent readers—readers who understand and respond to what they read and who are able to integrate and extend each new reading experience in a meaningful way. This understanding and response can only develop when children are engaged in reading texts which they find to be worth reading—because the readings are personally meaningful, entertaining, or enjoyable, useful in accomplishing some purpose, or represent a milestone of some kind to the reader.

The children whose work appears in this chapter were able to make effective choices and develop rich responses because they were engaged in activities that were important to them. They were able to make choices about the form their work would take; it is equally important that they were able to focus on developing meaning. Having initiated a frame of reference, they were able to pursue their ideas until they were satisfied with the result. For example, when Miya and Stina responded to the poems, they completed their representations relatively quickly in order to share them with their visitors; writing their novels, however, extended over several weeks.

Like Miya and Stina, all of the children and teachers we work with assume that reading, responding, representing, and sharing will make sense to them. Although they may struggle with some of the texts they read and the tasks they work on, the struggle is always toward **meaning** (rather than toward "correctness").

Although often students develop their own response tasks, we frequently ask them to work within a structure we provide, especially if they have been practicing or reviewing a particular strategy. We try to ensure that the tasks are open-ended and able to accommodate a range of learners and developmental stages. For example, working with a number of multi-age primary classrooms (our education system in British Columbia features ungraded, continuous progress during the first four years of school) we offered six response options for poems Miya, Stina, and other children were reading:

Listen-Read-Respond
Listen to the poem. Try to make pictures in your head. Tell someone about the pictures you saw. Read the poem yourself. Let new pictures come to your head. Show your ideas. You can write or draw.

Spider Webs
You are going to make a spider web of words, pictures, and ideas! Write the name of the poem in the middle of a blank

page. Circle it. Write some words or pictures it makes you think of. Make lines to join them to the name of the poem. Read the poem. Look for words in the poem that give you strong pictures or ideas. Add more words and ideas to your web. Show your web to a friend. Tell about it.

Partners in Poetry

Find a partner. Read the name of the poem together. With your partner, make up two questions about the poem. Read the poem together. Talk about your ideas: What parts did you like? Were your questions answered? Read the poem again. Decide how you will show your ideas. You can use both words and pictures. You might make a web or a cartoon. Work together to show your ideas.

I Noticed, I Wondered, I Liked

Read the poem. Close your eyes and let ideas come into your head. Read the poem again. You can write or draw on the page if you want. Tell one thing you noticed about the poem. Tell one thing you wondered about or wanted to know. Tell one thing you liked.

Take a Poem Home to Meet Your Family!

Find a poem you would like to take home to read with your family. Read the poem to someone in your family. Talk about your ideas and the pictures in your head. Remember to encourage other people's ideas. Let them read the poem to you. Work together to show your ideas in pictures or words. Write a notice together telling your teacher how you got along.

Show Your Ideas

Read the poem. Remember you can doodle or draw as you read. Think about the words and ideas. Read the poem over and over again. Show your ideas, feelings, and pictures. You can use words, pictures, cartoons, webs or anything you like.

Responses to all of these options can be connected to a rating scale similar to the one described in "Depth of Understanding" above. That would, of course, be determined by the teacher's purpose in providing assessment feedback.

Steven, who is eight, read the selection about the moon which prompted Stina to ask, "How did you get all this vital in-

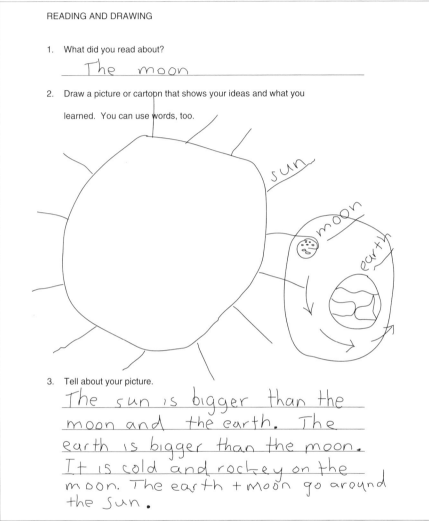

READING AND DRAWING

1. What did you read about?

    The moon

2. Draw a picture or cartoon that shows your ideas and what you

    learned. You can use words, too.

    sun

    moon

    earth

3. Tell about your picture.

    The sun is bigger than the
    moon and the earth. The
    earth is bigger than the moon.
    It is cold and rockey on the
    moon. The earth + moon go around
    the sun.

Figure 11 Steven's Reading and Drawing Response

formation?" Steven, however, brought quite different experiences and interests to the activity, and created meaning in a way that made sense for him (see Figure 11).

Steven is interested in how the universe works. He likes books about space and understands that some kinds of information are most clearly conveyed in a diagram. Steven spent quite a bit of time figuring out exactly how best to develop his diagram. He is pleased with the result: "Now I can show other people how the earth, sun, and moon move. My picture will help them understand when I explain it."

Readers and writers **do** work toward meaning. The kinds of trivial, artificial, and disconnected tasks that once masqueraded as "reading comprehension," were, in fact, unlikely to tell us anything about how young readers created meaning. This is because there was no real meaning to create—all too often, it was just a trick. On the other hand, when we invite children to participate in activities that make sense to them, we develop insights into both **how** they understand and **what** they understand of the world of print.

REFERENCES

Archbald, D. A., & Newmann, F. M. (1988). *Beyond standardized testing: Assessing authentic achievement in the secondary school.* Reston, VA: National Association of Secondary School Principals.

Brown, R. (1991). *Schools of thought.* San Francisco, CA: Jossey-Bass.

Brownlie, F., Close, S., & Wingren, L. (1990). *Tomorrow's classroom today: Strategies for creating active readers, writers, and thinkers.* Portsmouth, NH: Heinemann.

Brownlie, F., Close, S., & Wingren, L. (1988). *Reaching for higher thought: Reading, writing, thinking strategies.* Edmonton, AL: Arnold Publishing Ltd.

Jeroski, S., Brownlie, F., & Kaser, L. (1990a). *Reading and responding: Evaluation resources for your classroom.* (Vols. 1-2: Late primary and primary). Toronto, ON: Nelson Canada. (Available in the U.S. from The Wright Group, Bothel, WA.)

Jeroski, S., Brownlie, F., & Kaser, L. (1990b). *Reading and responding: Evaluation resources for your classroom.* (Vols. 1-3: Grades 4, 5, and 6). Toronto, ON: Nelson Canada. (Available in the U.S. from The Wright Group, Bothel, WA.)

Ministry of Education. (1991). *Thinking in the classroom: Resources for teachers.* Victoria, BC: Ministry of Education.

Nelms, B. F. (Ed.) (1988). *Literature in the classroom: Readers, texts, and contexts.* Urbana, IL: National Council of Teachers of English.

Perrone, V. (1991). *Expanding student assessment.* Alexandria, VA: Association for Supervision and Curriculum Development.

Smith, F. (1991). *To think.* Columbia, NY: Teachers College Press.

Authors

Robert H. Anderson is a professor at the University of South Florida, president of Pedamorphosis, Inc., Tampa, Florida, and co-author of *The Nongraded Elementary School* and *Nongradedness: Helping It to Happen.*

Kenneth Brown is a professor in the Foundations Division at the Faculty of Education, University of New Brunswick in Fredericton.

Faye Brownlie is a staff development consultant in British Columbia, specializing in teaching for thinking, active learning strategies, assessment, and cooperative learning. She has co-authored the book *Reaching for Higher Thought, Tomorrow's Classroom Today,* and *Reading and Responding—Evaluation Resources for Teachers.*

Kay Burke is vice president of instructional services for IRI/Skylight, in Palatine, Illinois and is a national presenter of staff development workshops. She is author of *What to Do with the Kid Who…: Developing Cooperation, Self-Discipline, and Responsibility in the Classroom* and *The Mindful School: How to Assess Thoughtful Outcomes,* and editor of *Authentic Assessment: A Collection.*

Carolyn Chapman is an international consultant and trainer in the Thomson, Georgia branch of IRI/Skylight. She is author of *If the Shoe Fits…: How to Develop Multiple Intelligences in the Classroom.*

Deborah L. Cohen is a staff writer for *Education Week*, Washington, D.C.

Donna Reid Connell is currently [1987] an independent preschool/primary reading/writing consultant. She has authored curricular materials put out by several major publishers. Dr. Connell has been an Early Childhood Education Consultant for the California State Department of Education; a school district Reading Specialist, Head Start Director, and kindergarten teacher; and director of a parent cooperative nursery school; and, for five years, Teacher-in-Charge of the Napa Valley, California Unified School District's Ungraded Primary School.

Charles DelForge is a graduate student at Western Carolina University pursuing a master's degree in elementary education.

Clarence DelForge is an Associate Professor of Elementary Education at Western Carolina University. His areas of expertise include combination classes, science, and classroom discipline.

Linda DelForge is an Associate Professor of Biology at Western Carolina University and is a graduate of Harvard University.

Jayne Freeman is now [1984] back to teaching a single-grade class—third grade, at Lowelling Elementary School in Milwaukee, Oregon.

Robin Fogarty is Creative Director with IRI/Skylight Publishing in Palatine, Illinois. She is author of *The Mindful School: How to Integrate the Curricula.*

Joan Gaustad received her B.A. in psychology from Grinnell College in Grinnell, Iowa, and her M.A. in clinical psychology from John F. Kennedy University in Orinda, California. She currently [1992] works as a freelance writer in Eugene, Oregon. She wrote *Schools Respond to Gangs and Violence,* the May 1991 OSSC Bulletin.

Yetta M. Goodman - is Regents Professor at the University of Arizona.

Chris Held is employed at Bellevue Schools in Bellevue, Washington.

Sharon Jeroski specializes in research, evaluation, and assessment at Horizon Research and Evaluation Affiliates, Vancouver, British Columbia. Author of several teacher resource books and student textbooks, she has also edited three collections of contemporary short stories for high school students.

Richard Lodish is principal of Sidwell Friends Lower School in Washington, D.C.

Andrew Martin is a retired professor in the Curriculum and Instruction Division at the Faculty of Education, University of New Brunswick in Fredericton.

Dennis Milburn (University of British Columbia Chapter of Phi Delta Kappan) is a professor of education and director of the Office of Field and Professional Development, University of British Columbia, Vancouver, [1981].

Bruce Miller is a rural education specialist in the rural education program at the Northwest Regional Laboratory in Portland, Oregon.

Randa Roen Nachbar, M.A., teaches a K/1 class at P.S. 11 Manhattan in New York City. She is also editor of *Day Care* and *Early Education* magazine.

John Newsom is employed at Bellevue Schools in Bellevue, Washington.

T. Marjorie Oberlander is director of elementary education for the Yakima Public Schools in Yakima, Washington. She was principal of the John Campbell School in Selah, Washington, [1989].

Barbara Nelson Pavan is Professor of Educational Administration, Temple University, Philadelphia, Pennsylvania.

Marian Peiffer is employed at Bellevue Schools in Bellevue, Washington.

David Pratt is Professor of Education, Duncan McArthur Hall, Queen's University, Kingston, Ontario, Canada.

Gina Rae is a resource teacher at Gilmore Elementary School in Richmond, British Columbia.

Linda Sartor is a sixth-grade teacher at Windsor Middle School, Santa Rosa, California.

Linda Schrenko is an educational consultant and is currently [1993] working with two nongraded pilot schools.

Robert E. Slavin is Principal Research Scientist at Johns Hopkins University, in Baltimore, Maryland.

Kate Sutherland is an apprentice, Findhorn Foundation Community, Forres, Scotland.

Kay D. Woelfel is principal of Marion Jordan Elementary School, Community Consolidated School District #15, in Palatine, Illinois.

Acknowledgments

Grateful acknowledgment is made to the following authors and agents for their permission to reprint copyrighted materials.

Section 1
The National Association for the Education of Young Children for "The First 30 Years Were the Fairest: Notes From the Kindergarten and Ungraded Primary (K-1-2)" by Donna Reid Connell, 1987, *Young Children*, 42 (5), pp. 30–39. Copyright © 1987 by the National Association for the Education of Young Children. Used by permission.

The National Association of Elementary School Principals for "The Dual-Age Classroom: Questions and Answers" by Kay D. Woelfel. From *Principal* vol. 71, no. 3, p. 32–33, January 1992. Reprinted with permission. Copyright © 1992 National Association of Elementary School Principals. All rights reserved.

Section 2
The National Association of Elementary School Principals for "The Return of the Nongraded Classroom" by Robert H. Anderson. From *Principal* vol. 72, no. 3, p. 9–12, January 1993. Reprinted with permission. Copyright © 1993 National Association of Elementary School Principals. All rights reserved.

The National Association of Elementary School Principals for "The Pros and Cons of Mixed-Age Grouping" by Richard T. Lodish. From *Principal* vol. 71, no. 5, p. 20–22, May 1992. Reprinted with permission. Copyright © 1992 National Association of Elementary School Principals. All rights reserved.

Section 3

From the Oregon School Study Council for "The Nongraded Classroom in Practice" by Joan Gaustad. From *Nongraded Education: Mixed-Age, Integrated, and Developmentally Appropriate Education for Primary Children,* p. 19–37, March 1992. Reprinted with permission. All rights reserved.

From Eric Clearinghouse on Rural Education and Small Schools for "Teaching and Learning in the Multigrade Classroom: Student Performance and Instructional Routines" by Bruce Miller, May 1991. Reprinted with permission. All rights reserved.

Skylight Publishing for "Nongradedness: Helping the Right Things to Happen to Kids" by Robert Anderson, "The One-Room Schoolhouse" by Robin Fogarty, "Multiple Intelligences: If the Shoe Fits" by Carolyn Chapman and Linda Schrenko, "Strategies That Work in Nongraded Classrooms" by Gina Rae, and "Parents: An Essential Part of the Learning Team" by Linda Schrenko. From *High Expectations Newsletter,* vol. 1, no. 2, Winter 1993. Reprinted with permission of IRI/Skylight Publishing, 200 E. Wood Street, Suite 274, Palatine, IL 60067. All rights reserved.

Section 4
From Randa Roen Nachbar for "A K/1 Class Can Work—Wonderfully!" by Randa Roen Nachbar, vol. 44, no. 5, p. 67–71, 1989. Copyright by Randa Roen Nachbar. All rights reserved.

The National Association of Elementary School Principals for "A Nongraded, Multi-Aged Program That Works" by T. Marjorie Oberlander. From *Principal* vol. 68, no. 5, p. 29–30, May 1989. Reprinted with permission. Copyright © 1989 National Association of Elementary School Principals. All rights reserved.

Section 5
From *Instructor* magazine for "How I Learned to Stop Worrying and Love My Combination Class" by Jayne Freeman. From *Instructor* magazine, vol. 93, no. 7, p. 48–54, March 1984. Copyright © 1984 by Scholastic, Inc. Reprinted by permission. All rights reserved.

The International Society for Technology in Education for "The Integrated Technology Classroom: An Experiment in Restructuring Elementary School Instruction" by Chris Held, John Newsom, and Marian Peiffer. From *The Computing Teacher*, vol. 18, no. 6, p. 21–23, March 1991. Copyright © 1991 ISTE. Reprinted with permission of the International Society for Technology in Education, Eugene, Oregon. All rights reserved.

The Canadian Education Association for "Student Achievement in Multigrade and Single Grade Classes" by Kenneth G. Brown and Andrew B. Martin. From *Education Canada*, p. 10–13, 47, Summer 1989. Reprinted with permission. All rights reserved.

The Education Digest for "The Consensus Classroom" by Linda Sartor with Kate Sutherland. From *The Education Digest*, January 1992. Reprinted with permission. All rights reserved.

Section 6
The International Reading Association for "Kidwatching: Observing Children in the Classroom," Yetta M. Goodman, *Observing the Language Learner*, Angela Jaggar and M. Trika Smith-Burke (Eds.), 1985. Reprinted with permission of Yetta M. Goodman and the International Reading Association. All rights reserved.

Skylight Publishing for "What Is a Portfolio?" by Kay Burke. From *The Mindful School: How to Assess Thoughtful Outcomes*, p. 44–49, 1993. Reprinted with permission of IRI/Skylight Publishing, 200 E. Wood Street, Suite 274, Palatine, IL 60067. All rights reserved.

Skylight Publishing for "How Do We Know We're Getting Better?" by Sharon Jeroski and Faye Brownlie. From *If Minds Matter: A Foreword to the Future*, p. 321–336, 1992. Reprinted with permission of IRI/Skylight Publishing, 200 E. Wood Street, Suite 274, Palatine, IL 60067. All rights reserved.

Index

There are

one-story intellects,

two-story intellects, and three-story

intellects with skylights. All fact collectors, who have

no aim beyond their facts, are one-story men. Two-story men compare,

reason, generalize, using the labors of the fact collectors as well as their

own. Three-story men idealize, imagine, predict—

their best illumination comes from

above, through the skylight.

—*Oliver Wendell*

Holmes